HOW TO START
A FAUX PAINTING OR
MURAL BUSINESS

A GUIDE TO MAKING MONEY IN THE DECORATIVE ARTS
Second Edition

REBECCA F. PITTMAN

ALLWORTH PRESS
NEW YORK

14 13 12 11 10   5 4 3 2 1

Published by Allworth Press
An imprint of Allworth Communications, Inc.
10 East 23rd Street, New York, NY 10010

Cover and interior page design by Natalya Balnova
Page composition/typography by Integra Software Services, Pvt., Ltd., Pondicherry, India

Library of Congress Cataloging-in-Publication Data

Pittman, Rebecca (Rebecca F.)
   How to start a faux painting or mural business : a guide to making money in the decorative arts / Rebecca F. Pittman.—2nd ed.
       p. cm.
Includes bibliographical references and index.
ISBN 978-1-58115-744-4 (pbk. : alk. paper)
1. House painting. 2. Texture painting. 3. Interior decoration firms—Management.
4. Small business—Management. 5. Home-based businesses—Management. 6. Interior decoration—Practice. I. Title.   II. Title: Guide to making money in the decorative arts.
   TT323.P58 2010
   747.068—dc22

                                    2010017904

Printed in Canada

I wish to dedicate this book to my mother, Collette Wells, for all the sacrifices, love, and support. For the sketchbook in my hand when I was eight, the microphone when I was nineteen, the tears of pride from the front row seats, and her unfailing belief that dreams are never out of reach, only languishing from lack of trying. I miss you more than I can say!

To Dad and Faye—there will never be a time I don't recall your love, support, and laughter.

To my beautiful departed sister-in-law, Vicki, who ran out to buy my first book the day it hit the bookstores and all the laughter we shared.

"It is one thing to be supported by those whose hands you can touch in your daily life, it is ethereal to know those who are no longer within reach are just as present as always."

CONTENTS

ACKNOWLEDGMENTS

The abundance that Life has left on my doorstep is staggering. I'm surrounded by people who care about me through the gray days and sunny ones. So, a big thank you to those of you who are waving the pom-poms over my humble accomplishments:

My four beautiful sons and their expanding families:

Mike—a paintbrush in one hand and physics book in the other; you amaze me. Thank you for your love, and your unfailing support. You are an incredible son, husband and father; I know Janel and Kaitlin are blessed to have you.

Brandon—you can make me laugh when things are darkest. Your optimism, sense of humor, and huge heart will always see you through; thank you for sharing them with me. Your accomplishments in the engineering field are just beginning. I am so proud of you and your beautiful wife, Kate, and children, Marek and Ashlynn. *You are appreciated!*

Casey—you light up a room and a stage. Thank you for sharing your own writing accomplishments with me. You are so very talented and have a brilliant future ahead of you! I am passing the quill on to you.

Ryan—my book buddy and all-star basketball player. Your wit and energy make me smile. "I'm so lucky" to have you in my life. Thank you for the love and laughter. I hope the world of Quantum Physics is ready for that brilliant mind of yours.

My beautiful daughters-in-law, Janel and Kate—you two should write a book of your own about your incredible artistic creations. Thank you for your love and for adding a feminine element to our home! I am so blessed to have two such beautiful and loving young women in our family.

To my effervescent grandchildren, Kaitlin, Marek, and Ashlynn. You are my Fountains of Youth and I adore the perspective you give me of the eternal childhood of Life. Thank you for making me laugh, imagine, and believe!

To my pom-pom wavers:

Jim, for all the love, support, and never-wavering friendship. You were there when things were the toughest. I owe you.

Marlena, my bubbly sister who is always so happy for me. I don't think we will ever grow up. Never Never Land has always held an allure for us. Thank you for your enthusiasm!

Mike and Scottie, my brother and soon-to-be sister-in-law. Thank you for the support and enthusiasm.

Gary Newman, Tom Dvorak, Todd Greene, Frank Farras, Garry Gronke, Richard Arnett, Walter Belling, Sondy Skrove, Shan Kleintz, Joe Martin, and many more who supplied support, enthusiasm and "hang in theres." I am truly blessed by your friendship and love.

Steve, Barb, Kendra (my artist buddy), and Dana Spanjer: You introduced me to your clients and inspired me with your work ethic and humor. Thank you so much!

Tad Crawford and the staff with Allworth Press for having faith in a new author. What a Thanksgiving and Christmas present. Thank you so much! You make it so easy to journey on this amazing career!

And, finally, to my mother, Collette Wells, who said, "If you want it badly enough, Becky, you'll achieve it!" You were there in the front-row seat for all the crazy things I've attempted in my life. I love and admire you more than you know. I still hear your voice inspiring me and pushing me forward. You are missed in my life every day. Thanks, Mom.

For all of you who took the time to write feedback on Amazon.com about the first book, you have no idea how much it meant to me to see that my little book had gone out and helped so many creative people go after their dreams. Thank you to those of you who reached me through the publisher with questions and thanks. It is truly my heart-felt pleasure!

INTRODUCTION

Thanks to the success of the first book, *How to Start a Faux Painting or Mural Business,* which was published in 2003, we are happy to bring you this second edition with updated information on all the new advances in the world of murals and decorative painting. This field has grown in extraordinary proportions, with more techniques, recipes, and avenues for creativity than anyone could have imagined. From a humble sponge to the plethora of faux finishing tools now offered, and from the first sketch to the detailed and imaginative murals that grace the walls and furnishings of businesses and homes throughout the world, the arena of decorative painting has exploded! So, without further ado...

Welcome to the creative world of murals and faux painting! Faux (the French word meaning "fake") took the world by storm over ten years ago and is still going strong. Where some critics claimed it would be a short-lived fad and wallpaper would soon be plastering walls once again, faux painting has continued to gain momentum and add to its gallery of options. Where once there was a simple sea sponge and glaze, we now find everything from troweled Venetian plaster, metallic and sand-imbued paint techniques, to stained cement and countertops. Add the individual style of the artist rendering these gorgeous finishes, and the field of creative possibilities is limitless.

You will find some new features in this book. I have added a special section in chapter 10 that breaks down all of today's faux finishes into the tools needed, strategies for bidding each of them, and any insights I can give you into understanding the time needed to complete each one. I have them subdivided into categories based on their similar tool usage, supplies, and time needed to render them. Feel free to tear this section out to carry with you when bidding your projects, but be easy on my book... I worked hard on this! You will also see a section for murals, frescoes, furniture, and decorative painting.

The supplies list has been expanded to contain today's latest tools and their capabilities.

You will find new information on using the Internet for everything from garnering research materials, to using the latest software for bookkeeping, to advertising your wares and hooking up with artistic workshops.

If you're one of the many creative people out there who desire to turn your love of paint into a lucrative business, this is the book for you. But, before we start, let me offer an insider's overview of this business.

True, you can make an incredible income in the faux painting and mural industry. True, naming your own hours and setting up shop in the comfort of your home or nearby shop is a great way to spend your days. True, the praise and excitement a client extends to you for a job well done is, to me, the best part of this career. But you need the following qualifications to succeed in this business:

- Dedication to the client and *his* needs. When you are at work on his project, the client's satisfaction is uppermost in your mind.
- Enthusiasm, which *is* contagious. You must really like people and enjoy brainstorming with them about their project. Go into an interview with a "You're just another paycheck to me" attitude and it will show. In chapter 4 we'll cover the importance of your personality and enthusiasm in the client's decision to go with you or someone else.
- Careful planning. This business requires careful scheduling of jobs, organizing your equipment and samples, and good record keeping.
- Good physical condition. Dragging ladders, scaffolding, and paint gallons around can be extremely tiring, as is standing, bending, and stretching for long periods of time.
- Understanding of color and its effect on its surroundings. You must also understand interior design themes, architecture, and lighting. Study the books out there on color theory and interior decorating.

- The artistic ability to render murals in a wide variety of themes and scales.
- A personality that can work with an infinite number of people, from contract laborers to the client.
- A desire to put in the hours and dedication necessary to learn today's latest painting techniques. Clients are more educated today on the latest trends in faux finishes and murals. Thanks to the multitude of television home décor shows, we have a knowledgeable audience who will want the newest and most innovative finishes. Please see chapter 10 for a list of some of the newest techniques. You will also find a list of workshops at the back of the book.

If you have these qualities along with the capacity to manage the financial end of things and you've put in hundreds of hours practicing the painting techniques so that you know your stipple brush from your chamois cloth, then you're ready to read on!

I have made my living as a muralist and faux painter for thirty-two years now. During that time I have met some incredible people. Clients have flown me across the country to paint their secondary and vacation homes, tossed me the keys to their golf carts, and stocked their refrigerators with my favorite soft drinks and nibbles. The things I prize most, however, are the thank-you cards sent in the mail or left on a client's kitchen counter along with a small gift of gratitude for making their home or business sparkle with their own personalities rendered in paint. Yes, it's been a lot of ladders, paint-spattered clothes, and sample boards. Would I have chosen another career...other than writing?

Not in a million years!

1

LAUNCHING A FAUX PAINTING BUSINESS

A decorative-painting career encompasses elements of house painting, interior decorating, and fine art. The person interested in starting a business in this area should have skills in all three or at least the willingness to learn about their techniques and requirements. This is not to say you must have a degree in interior design; however, understanding color, how light affects it and how it plays off other elements in a room, is essential in providing the client with a professional color selection. Hundreds of books on color and on mastering the techniques of faux finishes are out there. This book's intention is to teach the business end of this exciting career, not the art of faux finishing or murals.

Why the word "faux" when describing techniques of painting walls? Well, we've established that faux is French for fake. We are in the business of creating wall finishes that resemble other things: leather, suede, marble, Old World plaster, tortoiseshell, parchment, etc. So . . . now you can proudly tell your parents that you are embarking on a fake career!

Advantages of Choosing This Career

There are two huge advantages to starting a decorative painting career:

1. There is minimal start-up cost: business cards, building a portfolio, buying paint tools, small advertising costs, and perhaps vehicle lettering.

2. It is the type of business you can start on a part-time basis and from home. As all your business transactions will take place at the project site, there is no need to rent additional office space. An extra room or closet will suffice for an office and a little extra room in the garage or basement to store all your paints and tools will do just fine.

Among other advantages is that you will be looked upon as an artist—several steps above a typical house painter—and will therefore be expected to charge more. Clients are usually willing to wait a little longer to obtain your

services, since you specialize. I am typically booked ahead six months or more for painting jobs; sometimes as much as a year.

Walls are not your only canvas! Another perk to this expanding career is that the market for faux-finished furniture and accessories is at an all-time high. Exclusive furniture and gift stores are stocking room screens, furnishings, vases, pedestals, fabrics, and frames . . . all with hand-painted décor. You may be asked to paint floors to resemble cobblestone, a front door mimicking inlaid parquet (yes, I actually did this!), and a myriad other things your customer base dreamed up in the wee hours of the night. My favorite was being asked to paint Yosemite Sam with guns blazing on the back of a fishing boat with the lettering beneath him reading "BACK OFF!"

For these creative requests you will be well rewarded! You can expect to make anywhere from $280 to $1,000 a day, or more. The profit margin is extremely high as you are out only the cost of paint and some glazing medium on a typical faux project. Mural supplies are just as cost-effective when it comes to acrylic paints. Once you've made your initial investment in brushes, tarps, ladders, etc., you are banking an incredible income.

But along with the above-average income and naming your own hours comes a price:

- You are expected to know enough about interior decorating to recommend color and technique to a client who is sometimes "clueless"!
- If you are bidding a mural you will typically be asked for ideas about subject matter, scale, and color. You should be prepared to come up with your own designs and ideas if the client is not providing them. If hours of time will be dedicated to sketches, that time must be factored into your estimate.
- You must understand the effect of lighting on color and what the scale of the room dictates in terms of which color will "open it up" or "close it in."
- Some knowledge of architectural style is needed. You don't want to paint a rustic country mural or faux finish in a room that screams Georgian Revival.
- You must be able to wear a PR cap when dealing with a host of different personalities; from the client to construction workers who may be on site while you're there. Children must be dealt with, as well as pets. This is not for the thin-skinned!
- Extra time will be spent on going out to bid on a project you may not land.
- You must be able to present yourself and your portfolio with confidence, whether across a kitchen table of a homeowner or in a crowded conference room with a board of executives.
- The physical labor of hauling ladders and supplies in and out of job sites, crawling along floorboards, and dangling from ladders is tiring. This is not a desk job.

All the perks of the faux-finishing and mural business far outweigh any doubts you may have in the beginning. The best by far is the excitement shown by a client whose expectations have been met, or, better yet, exceeded! A job well done is the greatest feeling in the world. More than any other profession out there, the world of the decorative artist is filled with head-swelling praise. Your clients' looks of delight and exclamations of joy are enough to make you forget the huge paycheck that's coming . . . almost.

Becoming an Entrepreneur

Before we start setting up shop, just a few words about becoming your own boss. It's the American Dream to own your own business, right? Yes and no. The exalted feeling of creating a business with your name or logo on it and having it generate income is indeed heady. Being able to build a dedicated clientele due to your dedication and talent is wonderful. But if you think saying good-bye to punching a time clock and someone timing your lunch breaks equals total freedom, you might want to rethink becoming a one-man-show.

When you work for yourself, the buck stops here! You can't point to the next guy when something goes wrong and say, "He did it!" You are expected to be totally professional in your dealings with the customer and right any wrongs, repair any damages, and in some cases refund money. Instead of one boss, you now deal with as many as fifteen in one month . . . and the customer is always right! True, you tell the client what time you're coming and what time you're leaving. You may pencil in your child's flute recital on "company time" with no one to report to. But that same child may be sick, and you'll need to notify a client that a postponement of her project is necessary.

Children also interrupt your work time at home for myriad reasons, tie up your one-line phone, hog the computer, borrow your screwdriver, and take your new tube of Barn Red to school for a project without notifying you. (Obviously, these insights come from someone who's been there!)

You will always work harder for yourself than you will for someone else. Weekends are sometimes interrupted and some interviews will have to be conducted in the evening when the client who *does* work for someone else gets home. Whereas the typical workplace is free of children, pets, and vacuums, the decorative painter incurs all of these obstacles and more.

At one time I was rendering an Old World faux-finish eighteen feet off the ground at the top of an extension ladder while a floor carpenter installed hardwood boards beneath me and a two-man crew to my right continued fitting a fireplace insert into the wall I was working on. It was about this time the homeowner's cat sauntered past and narrowly missed stepping into my paint tray.

Recently I was in Maryland and DC painting wall murals in a series of pediatric dental clinics. Though the staff was amazing to work with and I miss them dearly, I can still hear the screams of little children as the dental drill approached their mouth! (Note: Aspirin should be on your supply list!)

Your health and insurance benefits must be handled by you instead of the benefit of a company's HMO being included in the package. If you're covered under a spouse's benefits, that's useful, but you'll still need the necessary business insurance. This will be covered in the next chapter.

Yes, you can generate more income this way than you would working for someone else. You set the standard and it's up to you to meet it. Your bank account reflects how hard you're willing to work and how many hours you spend bringing in new business. Chapter 3 covers everything you'll need to know about finding clients and getting those all-important referrals.

Obviously, even with all this information on the pros and cons of working for yourself, hundreds of creative people are entering the faux painting and mural arena every day with hopes of following their dreams: dreams of creating beautiful environments for their clients, dreams of owning their own business and setting up shop in their own home, dreams of having more control over their time and income. I'm one of them, and I'm happy to tell you that those dreams do come true and have made an incredible living for myself and my family. Part of that income was derived from painting murals, and I've included a chapter at the end of this book for those of you who would like to add murals to your repertoire. Most of the information offered in the upcoming chapters, however, applies to the mural business as well, so please don't skip this invaluable knowledge of the nuts and bolts of running a decorative painting career.

A word of warning is needed here: this is one arena where doors will open for your talents that you did not anticipate. Artistic skills are needed everywhere! Don't pigeonhole yourself unless you simply want to specialize and are happy camping in one campground. I have been asked to paint tire covers with company logos, illustrate books, do print work for advertising in magazines and newspapers, design logos, letterheads, and business cards, create signs, do calligraphy for wedding invitations, letter walls with prosaic verse, paint garage doors to look as if a Cessna is parked inside, create 3-demensional props for special events, design brochures, and even paint metal poles to resemble palm trees! You will be amazed at the creative gigs you will be offered. It really is wonderful and never boring. So be open to those moments where you hear opportunity knocking when you thought you knew who was showing up at your door!

While we are on the topic of unexpected opportunities being flung your way, it is always a good idea to keep researching, learning, and growing. Most community colleges offer courses in decorative painting, elementary art skills such as scale, perspective, and spatial awareness, as well as color theory and interior design. My library of art books is extensive. I typically buy two new bookcases a year to accommodate research materials, faux painting technique books, art books on every subject, magazines such as *Architectural Digest* and *Art World*, and much, much more. You can never know it all in this industry and the artist who keeps expanding his or her skills and offerings is the artist who is sought after for a fresh look or unique perspective on a project.

Another field of learning that may not have occurred to you is that of on-site education. I pay close attention to the electricians, drywall craftsmen, interior designers discussing spatial concerns with clients, interior painters, trim carpenters, etc. Why? By knowing the ins and outs of a new construction site ahead of time, I can recommend to the client the best time to have me come in to paint a faux finish or mural. For example, if I know that it will make my job easier to paint the wall before the carpet is laid and the baseboard is put down (eliminating hours of taping off baseboards and covering carpet with tarps), I can offer helpful suggestions that not only are pragmatic but make me look educated in the world of construction and timelines. By knowing typically when the electricians, trim carpenters, sound system people, etc. will be on site, I can make it easier for myself and for the client to schedule me when I won't be in the way of other craftsmen and vice versa. And most important, I can tell the client what base coat sheen I want used on the walls before the painters get to them and apply a flat sheen that will kill my finish or make my mural project harder due to the chalk-like, absorbent nature of that particular paint. I have also anticipated the dreaded "punch list"—the list of mistakes that new construction incurs. If there is something that has to be fixed on a wall I have already painted, I can think a few steps ahead as to how to fix the problem, or at least ask the project manager if they anticipate any problems cropping up on a wall that I have been given the go-ahead to paint. You would be surprised how many times someone has decided to add another outlet, change out lighting to track lighting (adding hardware where there wasn't any originally), or install surround sound speakers *after* I have finished a gorgeous wall! I don't know about you, but having a Bose speaker placed smack-dab in the center of my bottle-nosed dolphin's forehead kind of ticks me off! Stay ahead of the game, ask questions, and be alert!

A career in faux finishing, murals, and decorative painting is a fantastic way to make a living, make new friends, and have a feeling of control over your life!

So . . . let's get started with what you'll *need* to get started!

What You'll Need to Get Started

We will cover the legalities of opening a faux-finishing business in chapter 2. For now, let's begin with your other business needs. (Note that all of the upcoming information pertains to a mural business as well.)

Advertising Essentials

First, come up with a catchy business name. This area takes some real consideration, as your name will determine a number of things about your business. Most importantly, it will tell your prospective customers a little about who you are. If your name is Rag Works, because you thought it was a clever way to advertise ragging walls, the average guy seeing your name on your vehicle or in an ad might think you're a cleaning service. If you're trying to portray an elegant image rather than fun, you might lean toward something like Imperial Wall Glazes. If fun is your goal, you might come up with Glazed Over! Again, not everyone out there will know what you mean by *glazed,* and you may receive calls from customers ordering a dozen doughnuts. Using a name that doesn't come right out and identify the services you're offering requires a secondary line of explanation, such as Glazed Over! Decorative Wall Finishes and Stenciling.

Your business's name will also dictate where you fall in the yellow pages of your telephone directory. If having your name at the top of the list under Interior Decorators is important to you, then don't choose Walls R Us; something beginning with an A or B would be preferable.

This name you've selected will also need to convert readily to a logo. If your name is too long or spelled funny, you may have trouble designing an easily recognizable graphic. This logo will appear on your business cards, stationery, invoices, vehicle lettering, etc.; so take some time now to determine if you are giving up easy recognition for cutesy.

You will find out in chapter 2, under Registering, that the government office you apply to will search for any names duplicating the one you've chosen. It might be smart to come up with an alternate name or two in case the one you've chosen has been taken.

BUSINESS CARDS. You can have a local copier store, such as Kinko's, create beautiful cards for a small investment. Five hundred cards run roughly $150. Create a business logo or choose from one of the copier's stock images. Include your name and phone number at the bottom of the card. Include the secondary copy for *all* the services you offer in bullet form. For example:

FE FI FAUX FUM PAINTING
Faux Finishes · Murals · Stenciling
Jack Ladderman (555) 567-8910
Cell: (555) 522-5609 jklad@aol.com

Don't expect the client to ask, "So what else do you offer besides faux painting?" Having all your skills outlined on the card will ensure other bids in the areas about which clients would not otherwise have known.

You can also go to a reputable graphic design firm or print shop and order more expensive cards involving linen stock, embossing, etc. It all depends on your budget.

There are businesses online that offer bulk cards for little money. Shop around for one that looks reputable and has several templates to choose from, or better yet, does custom work. Make sure the shipping charges are clear up front. Some online stores make their money in bumped-up shipping and handling charges. Also look for ones that offer different font sizes. I recently ordered 500 cards and when they arrived the print was so small that anyone over 40 would need a magnifying glass to read them!

SELL SHEETS. A sell sheet is different from a typical brochure in that it is usually a single, two-sided, full-color sheet used to advertise your business. It is a great branding tool. It includes professional photographs of your best work, showing a range of techniques. If you have been interviewed for a prestigious magazine or organization, you can list that information here, as well as any awards or accreditations you might have. Your company information, Web site link, years in the business, and even customers' glowing reviews are great ways to convey you are not a flash in the pan and can be trusted to deliver a quality project. Personal testimonials from satisfied customers are hard to ignore and increase your perceived value, putting you ahead of the competition.

INVOICES. If you can afford it, have invoices from a print shop or graphic artist made up with your letterhead printed across the top. It makes a professional statement and so it is listed under advertising essentials. You can buy carbon invoices from an office store and write your name and phone at the top, but the impression will not be the same. If you have a computer with a good word-processing program or desktop-publishing software, you can print your own. Be sure you have at least a two-part carbon invoice . . . one for your record keeping and one for the client. Do not put your address on the letterhead of your business cards or your invoices if you work from home and prefer to keep your address private. The only time I give out my address to a client is when they need to mail in a payment or drop off samples of fabric, tile, etc., for a color match. Some home-based businesses rent a P.O. box for the small charge of $12 a month to use in their business dealings.

YELLOW PAGES ADVERTISING. In the beginning, I relied heavily on Yellow Pages advertising. Your ad is usually run under the heading of Interior Decorators. Some faux finishing artists also include their listing under Painting Contractors. There is also a section for muralists and fine artists. Take a look in your phone book under these listings for an idea of what others in your field are doing. A quarter-page ad can run as much as $280 on up per month.

To simply have your name listed with a phone number is usually $40 or more. To be honest, you won't get much from just a name listing. Customers look at the box ads first—and, sometimes, only. The box ads give you a chance to list your different services, plus a hook, such as "Free In-home Estimates." (Always a good one!) When you consider that one job landed from your Yellow Pages ad could net you $300 or more, it's a good investment.

FLYERS. My personal favorite. Delivering flyers to the exact doors in the exact subdivision you're hoping to target is the best bang for the buck. Create eye-catching flyers with desktop-publishing software (American Greetings Create-A-Card and Hallmark are good ones), then have them run off at a copier store.

> **TIP:** Save some money by creating only the text portion of your flyer on your computer. Then take the black-and-white text to a copier store, pick out a paper stock with a bright, full-color border the store carries, and have them run off a hundred or so. This saves you the cost of your color ink on your printer and allows you to deliver full-color, eye-catching flyers instead of black-and-white ones. You are in a very visual business, you know. Show it with color!
>
> A pack of twenty-five bordered sheets runs around $5.00. The copier's price to run off your text onto the in-store stock is roughly five cents to seven cents each, or $1.25 to $1.75 to run off 25 copies. When you add the $5.00 bordered stock charge, you get twenty-five full-color flyers—for under $7.00!

Hire a couple of energetic young people and drive them to your subdivision of choice. Have them hang the flyers on the door handles. Leaving them in mailboxes is illegal. Don't cut across lawns or flower beds. Avoid new homes with no lawn out front; their dollars will likely be put toward sod before paint, as most new subdivisions have a landscaping time frame included in the covenants. If you're targeting people with children for mural work, look for swing sets and basketball hoops.

DIRECT MAIL. For around $1,300, you can have a direct mail publisher print up and distribute roughly three to four thousand mailers to the area locations of your choice. You choose the street boundaries you wish your advertising to be delivered within and the company will mail your ads to the addresses falling inside those perimeters. You cover more houses than hand-delivering flyers, but your mailer is mixed in with the other mail and runs the risk of receiving only a quick glance before it is tossed into the trash. Compare also the cost of one hundred flyers run off at a copier's and hand-delivered to the houses of your choice for around $30 to the $1,300 spent on direct mail. Everyone will at least read a flyer stuck to their door; they don't always read junk mail.

VEHICLE LETTERING. Your local sign company can recreate your logo and cut it out in vinyl lettering for your vehicle. These letters are adhesive backed and stick to the car's body, or, my personal favorite, to the car's windows. All you need is your business name and phone number and a short description of your service:

FE FI FAUX FUM PAINTING
Decorative Wall Finishes & Murals
(555) 567-8910

I would recommend having your copy cut out of white vinyl if you're applying it to your windows. Windows have a dark tint and white shows up best. Have your sign person recommend a color for your car's body if you're lettering on the doors. Vehicle lettering serves two purposes: its gives you a professional look and it generates business. I have calls from people who say, "I was behind you at McDonald's Drive-Thru and wrote down your number. I need some walls painted!" (A Taco Bell or Burger King carries the same advantages!) The number of calls you'll get from your client's neighbors who rushed over to see what Mary Jane had done to her walls, because they saw your car with your name parked out front is well worth the cost of lettering, approximately $80 on up.

Today's sign shops offer full-color graphics that can wrap your entire vehicle in mind-blowing detail. The cost may be a bit prohibitive but the impact it makes is undeniable. Ask to see the latest in sign graphics for your car, van or truck.

> **TIP:** Remember, your name and phone number are now on your car. Keep it clean, tell the kids to avoid yelling at pedestrians when you're on personal errands, and be nice to the other drivers! (I once had my teenage son try to pick up a girl in the car next to us at a red light. Just a thought!) Car magnets are also available

Back window

for temporary use. The downside to magnetics is that they can be stolen and, if left on a vehicle door panel long enough, the area around the sign will fade, leaving a distinct outline in the car body paint where your sign has been. That's why I favor putting my advertising on the windows.

LETTERHEAD STATIONERY AND ENVELOPES. These are a form of advertising for your business as they convey an image of professionalism in all your correspondence. Itemized bids for commercial jobs can be printed on your letterhead stationery and submitted before the final invoice price is settled upon.

THE INTERNET. In today's world of technology, most businesses utilize the Internet in one way or another. Web sites can be designed and implemented from online set-up systems to store-bought programs. You can also pay a professional to design a bang-up one from $300 on up, depending on how many bells and whistles you want. We will have more to discuss about Web sites in chapter 3.

TRADE JOURNALS AND MAGAZINES. If you can afford the usually hefty price of putting your ad in a trade journal or magazine geared to your user market, it can be hit or miss. Usually a client will have to be actively searching for your services to notice the ads unless they are rather

GLAZED OVER!

3225 Nantucket Way

Waldorf, Maryland 56012

(555) 983-2406

The following bid is provided for faux finishing and mural work for the Peterson Medical Clinic at 3009 Bosum Way in Waldorf, Maryland:

1. Faux finishing in Amish Linen in 2-tone ragged in Waiting Area/all walls	$500
2. Faux finishing in Amish Linen in 2 tone ragged in Adjoining Hallway/all walls	400
3. Faux finishing in Sage Fields in color wash in Receptionist Area/all walls	300
4. Aspen mural with watercolor field landscaping in Receptionist Area/So. wall	800
5. Aspen trees in 3 stands in Public Bathrooms in West and East Wings	750
6. Faux finish in Sage Fields/color wash for Treatment Rooms 1-10 @ $400 ea.	4000
Total:	$6750

All finishes are in satin water-based paints. No ceilings are included in this bid.

A free touch-up service is provided for one year for minor scratches.

Project Date: September 19, 2004   Completion Date: October 2, 2004

Thank you for considering **Glazed Over!** Sketch of work area is attached.

large and prominently placed. You can approach these same magazines and request they run an article about your new business. If they are in need of filler or think your interview will enhance their publication, they may do the piece gratis. It never hurts to ask. You can also utilize these forums to search out people who are in similar businesses that might be good networking sources, such as people who remodel basements, offer interior painting, or interior designers and custom builders. There is a list of trade journals and magazines geared to the faux and mural industry under references at the back of the book.

WORD OF MOUTH will be your most effective form of advertising. Happy customers who show off their walls to friends and announce how pleasant you were to work with are an unequaled avenue for generating future business. Your promptness, attention to detail, quickly returned phone calls, and neatness will all be duly reported to everyone within earshot. Unfortunately, so will the derogatory comments!

NETWORKING is a huge way to promote your business and will be discussed in full in chapter 3.

Setting Up Shop

One of the many advantages of opening a faux painting business is the small start-up cost. You will need a place to call your office, even if it's a corner of a closet somewhere. Here's a list of things you'll need for your office setup:

DESK AND FILING CABINET. Keep it simple. You only need a place to sit and talk by phone to customers and utilize an organized filing system.

1. Clients: Files should be in alphabetical order and hold all pertinent information for each project, such as contracts, notes, color recipes, application technique, samples (if they will fit—if not label them and have them in alphabetical order on a shelf or in a large drawer with a note in the file stating where they are located), floor plans, copy of payments, etc.
2. Vendors: Keep another system with similar information for your vendors including payment receipts, purchase orders, dates, delivery scheduling, products, etc. If there are expiration periods on product specials, make a note of it.
3. Business Documents: Your business will have important papers that need to be kept in one place. These include your business plan, insurance policies, trade name license(s), DBA forms, bank agreements, etc.
4. Automobile records and mileage logs for your business use. I know keeping track of your mileage to and from a job site and for work-related purposes is a hassle, but you will need these numbers when tax time rolls around and will be grateful for the deductions.

5. Expenses: Keeping receipts of your business purchases for Uncle Sam is important. It is also a great way to keep track of your profit and loss in your business. If you notice you are spending more than usual on a job that is relatively the same size as a previous one, where is the extra money going? If the technique requires more expensive products, that's one thing, but if not, perhaps you need to go over where the money may be leaking out into unnecessary purchases or poor time management. Keep your check stubs from income and make sure that these files are divided into yearly categories.

6. Inspiration Files: I have many files of photos, ads, magazines pictures, postcards, greeting cards, fabric swatches, and imaginative business cards that I keep in my filing cabinet. The files are broken down into themes, such as wildlife, seascapes, children, fantasy, Tuscany, etc. for my mural business, and metallics, venetian plaster, wood graining, cement staining, etc., for my faux painting side. There are also miscellaneous files of projects and ideas that struck me as wonderful for future reference. I call these my Visionary Files. They never fail to inspire me to create something unusual and unique. They also come in handy as references to show your client when they can't quite decide what they want. By flipping through your files, they may see something that makes them smile and move in a different direction than where they had started. (Hint: ask before ripping out pages of magazines in the waiting areas of medical offices . . . they tend to frown on that. Ahem.)

7. Advertising: Keep a file of innovative advertising you have seen that you thought carried an impact for future reference and ideas. Keep copies of your ads and those of competitors and refer to them often. If you have placed ads, keep records of your rate sheets, contracts, deadlines, and run times.

8. Clients Pending: These are people you have talked to and may be working with at a later date. The retail industry calls them "be backs." Give them a follow-up call after a little time has passed, just to keep your name on their mind. Do not hound them or it will do the opposite of winning them over. Something I have used that is effective is a polite, brief call to let them know some time has

opened for me that I had not expected by clients pushing a date out, a construction delay, etc. I ask if they would like to take advantage of that opening. I keep it light and friendly and thank them for their time if they are still undecided. I'm not big on the hard sell . . . I don't like it when it's done to me and I don't know of many people who appreciate being badgered and coerced.

Set aside a drawer or shelf to hold all your sample boards, faux finishing books, magazines, etc.

COMPUTER. A computer nowadays is almost a necessity. I use mine to keep track of appointments, type out itemized bids, design advertising packages, and correspond with clients. Today's software also includes record keeping systems, spreadsheets, invoicing, and accounting and payroll systems that can actually interface with your accountant or bookkeeper. You can pay bills online and keep track of your expenditures. The Internet is also an endless source of decorating ideas and supply stores. Many of your commercial clients will prefer the speed of e-mail over traditional mailing options. Web sites, blogging, and workshops are also new sources to advertise your business and keep your name prominently in the forefront.

PHONE AND ANSWERING SERVICE. If you're going to be in business, you'll need a way for clients to reach you while you're out decorating. If you're using a voice-mail feature with your phone, leave a professional and brief message asking for information. Working from your home can have disadvantages when it comes to the phone. If you have only one line, it must be shared with the rest of the household. Call waiting is a must if you don't want to miss calls while your son Mathew ties up the phone as he describes in detail to a friend how Suzanne Phelps dumped him during third-period history class. Return calls promptly! Customers shop around and may have bid the job to someone else by the time you get around to calling back. Promptly returning calls when notified of problems from a job you've completed are more important still! Consider getting a second phone line that is for your business only. It is not expensive and could save your business, your nerves, and your marriage! If you have a second line added for your business, it will be listed in the phone directory as such and will cost a little extra, usually in the neighborhood of an extra $35 a month. To me it was worth it and added a professional touch to my home-based business.

Today, everyone has a cell phone. It's up to you if you want to use your cell phone as your business phone number. I do not. The last thing I need while hanging from a ladder or having hands filled with paint is to have to answer an incessantly ringing phone. I prefer to have a landline with a professional voicemail set up. I check the calls periodically during the day and call only those who can't wait until I return to "the office." It's your call.

FAX MACHINE/COPIER/SCANNER. Commercial clients will ask for information to be faxed to them or will want to fax changes and updates to you. Get a fax machine that has a copier to save money. *Always* keep a copy of your correspondence, bids, and drawings. It avoids misunderstandings down the road and gives you a ready reference to consult when memory fails you. A color copier is a must in this business. It comes in handy when printing out full-color reference materials to show the client or to use for murals, etc. You can also print your own flyers, brochures, sell sheets, and business cards in color and print out photos of your work on glossy photo stock. A scanner can be used to scan material into your computer that can then be used in e-mails, Web sites, and other Internet-related functions. They also come in handy when scanning material that needs to be faxed. Many copiers come with a scanner included.

CELL PHONE. Advantages of a cell phone are obvious. If you're running late, you can phone ahead or ask for directions if you've already circled their block several times. Mine brings me peace of mind, since I know that, if an emergency arises at home, my family can reach me. I do inform my clientele that, due to the nature of my business, I prefer they use my office number as a means of reaching me, as mentioned above.

OFFICE SUPPLIES. You don't need much in the way of supplies for your office: letterhead stationery, invoices, a Rolodex of client information, pens, paper clips, file folders, and printer supplies. Folders for each client's information is a must and extra ones for vendors and supply invoices. Software to keep ledger records or the latest in Photoshop and other art-related tools can be added to your computer.

> **TIP:** For a quick reference you can keep track of your clients' projects on the back of the Rolodex cards bearing their names. I usually write the name of the paint I used in their project(s) and which room it was for. This information is also on their invoice in a file folder, but I find the Rolodex system useful when I'm making

a quick call or receiving one. With today's obsessive need to use our comput-ers, Blackberries and cell phones for logging information, I still use a good old Rolodex as a back-up. Call me crazy but there are times when computers crash, cell phones are lost, and Blackberries are left in the golf cart.

CAMERA. Lots of pictures! You'll need them for your portfolio, for ref-erence pictures, or to capture ideas at home shows, etc. If you have a digital camera, so much the better. You can print out your own copies on your printer in the comfort of your own home and manipulate them with today's great software on your computer. Create brochures, mailers, Web sites etc., showing off your work! We'll talk more about photos in chapter 3, Building Your Portfolio.

Your Supply Storage

You will need an area to store your paints, tarps, paint tools, etc. A section of the garage works fine for storing most of your materials. If you live in a state where the temperature falls below 40 degrees, you'll need to store the paint and sponges indoors. Sponges retain moisture after a job and will form crys-tals if left in cold temperatures. This causes the sponge to become brittle and fall apart. Paints can be ruined by the cold, so take good care to protect them.

Organize your supply area so that everything is right at your fingertips. Eliminate stress and get to your tools quickly by having tarps, sponges, rags, brushes, ladders, and other supplies in their own area. I use the clear plastic storage bins sold at department stores to store individual items; foam brushes in one, rubber stamps in another, and so forth. Sharpened pencils, large eras-ers, and markers are kept in their own unit. I have a paint kit that travels with me everywhere. It includes a tape measure, screwdrivers (both flathead and Phillips, to remove light-switch plates), a paint key (to open cans), plumb line (or the new laser levels are marvelous!), pencils (a contractor's mechanical pencil sold at hardware stores is wonderful . . . no more sharpening), large erasers, notepad (to leave notes to myself and to the client), thank-you notes to leave behind, paint shields, rags, craft knives, denatured alcohol, misting bottle, dust masks, paint trays, paint rollers, edgers, blank sample boards, cheesecloth, string and push pins (for drawing large circles), halogen light, extension cord, tracing paper, masking film, clear acetate, extra paper towels, vinyl spackle (to patch nail holes), sandpaper, my artist brush kit (fine-line brushes come in handy for small areas and along ceiling lines) my car keys, cell phone, snacks, and stencil adhesive spray. Both regular masking tape and the blue 3M painter's tapes are always loaded in this kit. If you want to really score points, take along some little diversion for kids, such as coloring books and crayons, small puzzles, etc. Purchase a large plastic craft tote with handles for a handy carrying kit to include all of the items mentioned above. Anything with handles is a welcome way to haul things in and out.

One of my favorite carriers for the job site is a 3-drawer plastic cart on wheels that you can find at most department stores. The flat surface holds paints, reference books, etc., while the pull-out drawers keep all your supplies in handy, reachable areas, and best of all, you push it around rather than carry it. It keeps your area tidy and neat instead of tubes of paint littering your tarps or tabletops. You can also hide a snack inside or your cell phone, extra paper towels, and your business cards. It can be rolled out to the car and placed easily inside.

A list of painter's supplies is provided at the back of this book. However, it should be mentioned here that you will need room for at least four different-sized ladders: a six-foot step-ladder (aluminum is lighter and easier to move around), an eight-foot step-ladder (fiberglass is better here, for more support), an eighteen-to-twenty-foot extension ladder, and an articulated ladder for stairs, scaffolding, and hard to get at places. A two-step utility ladder comes in handy when reaching low areas and to sit on for murals and fauxing half-walls.

All other supplies are usually small and easy to store, with the exception of some of the larger buckets, yardsticks, Ahl sticks, etc. Keep your tools clean, in good repair, and within easy reach.

You will end up with a huge supply of art brushes. Choose quality brushes. The cheap ones will only fall apart, lose their edge, and shed. Nothing is a frustrating as picking shed hairs from your work as you watch your brush self-destruct. To clean acrylic paint out of brushes, soak the brushes for at least an hour in rubbing alcohol, and then wash with Murphy's Oil Soap and a plastic brush scrubber. The types of brushes you will be need are listed in the supply section at the back of the book.

You will be replacing sea sponges regularly; they wear out from covering knockdown textures on walls and scraping across paint shields. Most sponges run $8 to $14 each. Keep them in open re-sealable plastic bags between jobs. Keep all lids on paint cans securely fastened; air will thicken the paint, and dirt particles will find their way in.

> **TIP:** Make a master sheet to hang on a clipboard near your paint gallons. On this sheet list the name of the client and the paint color with a number. In black marker, number each gallon to match the correct name and number on your master sheet, i.e., Mary Roberts/Buttersquash Yellow/2.

All artists have their special way of doing things. Some decorative painters like to use large plastic cups attached to ladder tops with tape or Velcro strips to hold their paints, brushes, pencils, erasers, etc. to eliminate several trips down the ladder.

Some use disposable paper palettes for smaller projects like stenciling or some simple decorative art. I use a regular paint tray when painting murals as I am working on large wall areas and a small palette would not allow me to mix the mass quantities I need. I also like that as the acrylic paints dry in the tray, the whole thing can be peeled out in one rubbery mass and the tray is good as new and ready to go again. It is also easy to balance on my lap if I am sitting while painting a mural.

Faux painting usually requires buckets, although some techniques utilize paint trays. A good idea when using paint from a can is to place it inside a larger can or bucket to catch the drips from your brush, rag, sponge, or whatever. Glazes can be messy and this simple tip will save you a lot of headaches and clean-up.

A paint hook to hold your paint cans while painting on a ladder is another great idea, and always have a paint rag or paper towels up there with you.

I tend to wear an apron with pockets to hold small rags, pencils, tape, erasers, etc.

If you care about your hands, wear latex or nitrile gloves. There are a number of gloves on the market, especially those used by medical professionals that will fit snugly enough to allow you do intricate detail work, and keep your nails and skin from looking like you just graduated from the Car Mechanic's Academy! The nitrile gloves are heavier and won't melt when using solvents and oils. Keep a box of them on hand . . . no pun intended.

That's about all you'll need to get started. If money's short, don't worry! One of the great aspects of opening a painting business is the fact that supplies can be bought as needed. You'll be receiving a deposit for each job, and the supplies for that job are purchased with the deposit money. Obviously, larger items such as ladders and tarps will need to be accounted for ahead of time; all other items required for a specific job, such as paint, sponges, and tape, can be purchased as the need arises. Keep your receipts in case the client wants to see what you spent on his job and check that you weren't buying more supplies than his project required. You will also need them for tax purposes.

Your Work Area at Home

We have discussed having an area for your office needs, but artists require a work area. Though the majority of your work in the faux painting and mural realm will be done on a job site, you will still need a work table, good lighting, heat, and supplies near at hand when rendering sample boards, painting furniture or floor cloths, portable room screens, hanging art, portraits, 3-D art, and any number of fun projects that may come your way. I have designed and painted many objects that I created from wood, so my work area included saw horses, jigsaws, table saws, sanding equipment, drills, and hardware. It is totally up to you how far you want to expand your business. My sons used to hurry home from school with their friends in tow to find an eight-foot-tall Frankenstein in the garage made of plywood, or a children's pirate fort. I will admit, the Frankenstein gave my neighbors pause, but I was never boring!

This is your work area, so surround yourself with things that make you happy and relaxed. Have your CD player or radio hooked up, a small refrigerator with your favorite cold drinks or snacks, inspirational posters or messages posted on the walls, a calendar with your project dates, and a large dry erase board listing upcoming jobs, workshops, or special events. If you are using a garage or basement, make sure the area where you will be doing most of the sitting or standing is heated or has a cushioned area beneath you to protect your feet from the hard, cold surfaces. Make sure you have ventilation when working with solvents, varnishes, oils, etc. If you are sanding, wear a dust mask and use a tack cloth to make sure your surfaces are free of sawdust.

Alert your family and friends when there is wet work drying in your work area. Having someone open the garage door on a windy day just when you finished base coating a dresser is not going to make you happy. Keep pets away for obvious reasons. Your family needs to be team players when it comes to your work environment. Post a sign on the doors leading to your workshop that says, "Stay out ...Wet paint and project in process!"

Having a phone handy to eliminate trips to the main house is always nice, and caller ID is a must!

Your Portable Office: Your Car

To go out and render works of art on blank walls requires a number of tools. Ladders, tarps, buckets, your paint kit, paints, brushes, etc. all need a lot of space. Today's SUVs, minivans, trucks, and station wagons can haul a lot. I drive an SUV and have packed as many as three ladders *inside* (including one eighteen-foot extension ladder!) and filled the back with all the necessary paint tools for a job. It is my portable office and studio. This "office" needs to be just as organized, if not more so, as your in-home setup. Customers often get a glimpse of your car's interior, and, if it looks like a football practice was just held inside, this does not reflect well on you. There have been many times when kind-hearted clients have offered to help me pack equipment in or lug it out and have commented on how organized my car setup was. Here are some great tips to help you maintain an organized portable office.

Organizing Your Car

- Place a wooden crate or a carton in the back of your vehicle to hold paint cans. This keeps cans from accidentally spilling.
- Have your plastic containers handy, with your foam brushes, sponges, and pencils.
- Tarps should be neatly folded and stacked; always shake them out between jobs.
- Keep reference materials such as magazines, books, photographs, etc., stacked in a box or in a file folder.
- Have a bucket or carton of rags, cleaning solvent, and a heavy-duty stain remover, such as Goof Off, handy in case of accidental spills.

- All invoices and paperwork should be organized in a file folder.
- Have a small vacuum such as a Dust Buster to vacuum up sponge crumbs, etc. This will prevent you from leaving the client with small debris. A whisk broom and pan is a good idea as well.
- Finally, keep your car vacuumed and clean. Pulling up in a dirty vehicle gives the wrong impression, as does an interior cluttered with fast-food wrappers.

By all means take along a lunch, a CD player, and anything else that will make your workday pleasant. Ask the clients if they would object to some *quiet* music or your use of earphones. Some people feel earphones are rude and intimate that you don't want to be bothered. Include in your "must-haves" a box of disposable booties, the kind found in medical stores. Many of the homes scheduling your services will be brand new. Owners expect shoes to be removed. Since climbing ladders in socks is painful, booties worn over your shoes is a respectful acknowledgment of their house rules.

One final word about your vehicle. Always ask if you are in the way if you park in the driveway. Before I start unloading things, I usually ring the doorbell and ask if where I've parked is convenient. If your car leaks oil, by all means, park out on the road.

Now that we've covered your initial startup needs, let's move on to the fun stuff . . . the IRS and insurance coverage!

2

FIRST THINGS FIRST

You want to own your own business? Great! Do you want to be a one-man-show or would you prefer to have a partner to help with the financial setup and hold the ladder for you? There are three categories that a new business must choose from to set up a company legally: sole proprietorship, partnership, or corporation.

Sole Proprietorship or Partnership?

You will need to decide which structure you will be flying your new flag under. Now is the time to decide whether you enjoy your own company or if you would prefer to have someone else in on all the fun. Let's look at each one.

Sole Proprietorship

If being the captain of your own vessel and keeping all the profits hidden under your private poop deck is the only way you envision running a business, then sole proprietorship will be the box you check at the top of your business forms. On days when you're not feeling well, or the car breaks down, or little Harry has the chicken pox, you will have to call clients affected by your delays and make things right. You will order the paint, clean the brushes, buy the insurance, fix the "ugly spot" on the perfect wall you just painted yesterday, and fill out the income tax forms. The upside is you're not waiting around for the partner who has a hard time getting out of bed in the mornings or fighting over who's going to deal with an irate customer *this* time. There is a sense of freedom when you have only yourself to manage. There is also the burden of knowing everything depends on your capabilities . . . or lack thereof.

DBA, "Doing Business As"

If you like the idea of being a sole proprietor, the most common way to set up your business is as a DBA—a Doing Business As account. You will first need to contact your local Small Business Administration office to find out what the licensing requirements are for your city and state. They vary widely from area to area, even within the same state. Ask what licenses you will need to open a home-based business. Many vendors, interior design wholesalers, and other entities will require that you have a business license in order to do business with them.

File a DBA form with your local county Registrar, noting that you are the owner of the business. This form or your newly acquired license will be needed in order to open a bank account for your business. Most banks will simply go online to the Secretary of State listings to see if you have been certified as a working entity under the name you want printed on your checks. If you are not listed, or if your business name has expired, you will need to reinstate it for a small fee, usually under $20. Filing for a DBA with the registrar will cost around $75 to $100, which is a one-time fee. Make sure you keep it current, however, as it will need to be renewed yearly. You can do this online at *www.sos.state.__.us/*. In the blank, type your state's two-letter abbreviation. For instance, I'm in Colorado, so I would type *www.sos.state.CO.us/*. You can also contact your local Secretary of State.

I would highly recommend finding a good accountant at this point. Accountants are invaluable in telling you your particular state's requirements for new businesses, tax filing stratagems, how the IRS prefers to have a sole proprietorship file and how often, and just some good recordkeeping advice. There are some pretty stringent rules for tax deductions for a home-based business that we will cover later.

Partnership

If you are considering a partnership, I highly recommend having a partnership contract drawn up by an attorney. Yes. I know he's your best friend from high school and you've never had a single argument in your life and you'd trust him with your pet ferret . . . however, business deals are a whole new ball game. Let money enter the picture, and friendship has a way of taking a long vacation. With a legal contract drawn up, any and all of the remote possibilities of disagreement are covered. You may want to hire more employees down the road, and your partner may want to keep it a cozy twosome. You may have done 65 percent of the work on a huge project because your partner had a root canal done during the last two days on the job, but he still feels he should get 50 percent of the profit. Perhaps the two of you can't agree on how much to spend on liability insurance or whether to dig into the coffers and buy that new scaffold setup. If you have a partnership contract, all the i's and t's would be dotted and crossed ahead of time. Worst-case scenario, one of you wants to buy the other one out, or you two have a dispute that can only be settled in court, the agreement will have the format already laid out. Partnership insurance will protect you against any lawsuits your best-friend-turned-partner may levy against you.

The benefit of having someone share the business is obvious. Two sets of hands can paint a room twice as fast as one; you have someone to talk to, who can also talk to the homeowner or businessman so that you're not always on call. Loading and unloading equipment is faster and less fatiguing and *he* can take the twenty foot-high ceiling this time! You split the responsibilities and the income. If your partner shines at closing a deal and you sparkle at preparing professional-looking sample boards, it's a good balance. Perhaps you're the faux painter and she's the mural artist. However, if she prefers to start work at 6:30 A.M. and you're more an 8:45-ish kind of person, a compromise will have to be reached. The objective is to find someone who offsets your weaknesses and complements your strengths.

Some things you will want to discuss with your partner when deciding what to put in the contract are:

- Who will be in charge of setting up and maintaining the company bank account? Will both be privy to the checkbooks and credit cards?
- Will one person be in charge of buying and/or storing supplies? If supplies are spread out between two houses, it can get confusing. "I thought you brought the 3M tape!" "No, you said

YOU were bringing it!!" Try to keep supplies in one area, neatly organized.

- How will you and your partner handle the tax situation? Who keeps the records, receipts, mileage, etc.?
- Who handles the contracts, paperwork, billing, etc.?
- Whose address and phone number will be used for the business and advertising?
- If the partnership should dissolve, who will keep the assets, inventory, etc.?

Keep in mind things do happen to end a partnership. One partner may simply move away. Get all the details in writing and you just might save your business and your friendship.

Corporation

The plus side to setting your business up as a corporation is that the corporation, not you personally, will be responsible for debts incurred. Corporate tax laws are complicated, and you will probably need a CPA to explain them to you. If someone should bring a lawsuit against you, it will be filed against the corporation and its assets rather than your personal ones. You have a little more privacy as you stay in the shadow of a corporate umbrella, and your letterhead will reflect the corporate logo and mailing address. Initial fees are higher and, in my opinion, not worth it to a small business specializing in faux finishes and murals. The financial layout for supplies and equipment is pretty minimal, and the liabilities not on the same scale as, say, an interior design company, which is responsible for carpet, fabric, window coverings, and expensive inventories.

Registering

We talked about registering your new business earlier when discussing a DBA. When filling out the form you will be listed as a *service*, not retail. The form is #5092 and can be downloaded from the Internet at *www.revenue.state.___. us*. Fill in the blank with the initials of your state—e.g., *www.revenue.state. co.us* if you live in Colorado. If you'd like to check the Internet yourself to see if anyone else out there has selected your business name for their own, go to *www.businesstax.state.___.us*. Again, fill in the blank with the initials of your state.

While you're registering your company name, ask how to file quarterly for income tax (more about income tax later in this chapter). You can ask that quarterly forms be mailed to you.

Federal ID Number

You will need a Federal ID Number if you plan to hire employees. If you have decided to go it on your own, your social security number will suffice whenever you are asked to supply a Federal ID number on forms or over the phone. Down the road, if you do take on additional help, you must request this number.

Tax Resale Number

You are actually charging your client for two separate things on an invoice: your services (labor and talent) and the price of the materials used on the job. You charge tax on the materials *only*, not your services. Because you are charging tax on the materials that you resell, you should not pay sales tax to merchants from whom you buy them. You will need to register your tax resale number with the merchant in order to avoid paying sales tax twice (to the merchant, and to the government). Break down the materials on your invoice (paint, sponges, tape, etc.) and charge the applicable city and state tax percentage on your invoice. Some businesses that offer both service and product keep their tax profits in a separate account so that it is available at tax time and not accidentally swallowed up in the business. You will need a Tax Resale Number and will go to your local tax collector's office to obtain one. They can give you quarterly payment forms. Be sure and keep careful track of your taxes and pay them in a timely manner.

Setting Up Your Bank Account

Take your newly acquired trade registration form with you to your bank and apply for a commercial account. If you are starting out small, you can combine your personal account with your business into a d/b/a account. D/b/a simply means "doing business as." For instance, if your name is James Windell, your checks would read James Windell d/b/a Fe Fi Faux Fum Painting, and then list your address and phone information. While this may save money on maintaining two separate accounts, the downside is that it is easier to dip into your business revenue for personal purchases. A separate account also makes it easier, come tax time, for you or your accountant to figure out your P & L (profit and loss statement). Pass on the checks with the cutesy ducks and puppies background for your business. Keep your checks simple and professional.

Insurance Needs

There are several kinds of insurance coverage you must have if you're in business. First, take a look at how much you have invested in equipment and supplies. A typical homeowner's policy will only cover roughly $2,500 to $3,000 of business equipment kept in your home. If you want additional coverage, you must purchase property insurance for equipment at home and business property insurance to insure equipment while in use away from home.

Health insurance is alarmingly expensive when obtained for a one-man-show. If you're married and are covered under a spouse's coverage, then you can forgo this expense. Check with insurance agents and ask about group rates and discounts.

Life insurance is a way of protecting your loved ones should you and your business no longer factor into their financial picture. It gives you a feeling of security and peace of mind.

Liability insurance is the most important coverage a small business owner can carry, especially if he's out in the world dangling from ladders and moving equipment and paint around in a million-dollar home. This insurance will cover damages incurred when your ladder accidentally comes into contact with their plate-glass mirror. One of my favorite sayings is from *Man of La Mancha* and it applies to this scenario: "Whether the stone meets the pitcher or the pitcher meets the stone . . . it's going to be bad for the pitcher!" So, whether their mirror ran into your ladder or your ladder ran into their mirror, bottom line is, the mirror is broken and the owner is looking at you with one eyebrow raised (never a good sign!). Liability will also cover misfortunes at your office site should, for any reason, a client be there and sustain an injury.

General liability insurance for $500,000 to a million will run roughly $1,300 a year at the time of this printing. These rates tend to rise each year, so check with your agent. A plus in having this much coverage is that some commercial jobs will require you to be insured for that amount, and, if you can produce proof of coverage, you have a leg up over the other guy who doesn't. The premiums will need to be paid quarterly. If you subcontract any labor from other artists or contractors, make sure they carry their own coverage.

Auto insurance is something I'm sure you already carry but ask about coverage if you are in an accident while at the job site.

Disability insurance is your safety net in the event you are injured or out of work for reasons beyond your control. Your insurance will pay a portion of your average salary for a set period of time. This is where your careful record keeping comes in handy. The insurance company can see by your commercial bank records, P & L's, etc., what you typically earn and compensate you accordingly. For a sole proprietorship, this is a must!

In my twenty-three years of experience as a decorative painter, I have never once been asked if I were bonded. Being bonded gives the clients the peace of mind knowing that if the job is messed up or not completed on time, the bond will protect them and their investment. Some builders and commercial jobs will require that you provide proof of this coverage.

Find a good agent and acquaint him with all aspects of your business. The more he understands your services and typical clientele, the better he'll be able to facilitate your insurance needs. If you are not carrying renter's or homeowner's insurance, get rates on those as well.

The Business of the Faux or Mural Business

It's IRS time! Operating your home-based business comes with paperwork. The one thing you'll miss about working for someone else is having the majority of your tax concerns taken care of. Your former employer withheld federal, state, and perhaps city taxes from your paycheck, as well as Social Security and Medicare (FICA). It also paid unemployment taxes (FUTA). All these are reported on a W-2 form.

But, no, you wanted to do it on your own. So . . . here you go! You will need to pay income tax on your net profit and pay self-employment tax, which covers Social Security and Medicare. You will pay sales tax based on your supplies and materials charged to the client. Check with your local government agency to determine what the tax demands are in your area; they vary. For an overview of what the federal government requires, you can go online to *www.irs.ustreas.gov.*

The IRS has a Tax Guide for Small Business (Form 334) that will help you with your Schedule C or Schedule C-EZ. You will need to choose from these two forms for your home-based business and attach it to Form 1040. This tax guide will help you determine your tax year, accounting, cost of goods sold, and gross profit and business expenses.

Schedule A lists personal deductions and must also be filled out. (Are we having fun yet?) If you were a subcontractor for another business, you will be issued Form 1099-MISC at the end of the year.

You will send in quarterly income tax and must estimate what you feel you will earn in one year. Always err on the side of generosity here or you'll owe Uncle Sam come April 15. If you think you could possibly gross $65,000 before April 15, then divide that by four and mail off your payments based on that amount . . . on time! The IRS has a helpful publication for this area as well: Form 505, Estimated Tax Payments. These quarterly payments are due April 15, June 15, September 15, and January 15. Form 1040-ES has an Estimated Tax Worksheet to help you figure how much you might expect to pay. A good rule of thumb is to set aside between 15 to 28 percent of your gross income to handle your projected tax liability.

Let's take a look at what you can claim on your income tax forms. As someone who is self-employed, you will be required to fill out the specific forms we just went over for Uncle Sam. Here are some expenses you may be able to claim.

Fixed Expenses

If you are working out of your home, you are able to claim certain things as deductions on your Income Tax Self-Employed Forms. These include:

RENT. The area of your home used *exclusively* for your painting business (such as office, portion of basement, or garage) can be deducted from the total yearly price of your rent or mortgage payment. Figure out the square footage of these areas used and determine what percentage of your home's square footage is set aside for business purposes *only*. For instance, if your home is 1,000 square feet and the room used exclusively for your home-based business measures 10' × 10' (100 square feet), then the percentage of space used for business purposes is 10 percent (1,000 divided by 100). Use that percentage as the number for determining your mortgage or rent portion used for business endeavors. Form 8829, Expenses for Business Use of Your Home, is there to help you with your calculations.

> **TIP:** You cannot claim the dining-room area simply because you sit at the table there and do sample boards or talk to an occasional client; the area claimed must be used solely for business purposes and nothing else.

PROFESSIONAL FEES. Accountants, lawyers, money paid for special classes, a professional's advisory fees, a photographer's services, etc.

ADVERTISING AND PROMOTIONAL COSTS. Car lettering, Yellow Pages ads, flyers, newspaper ads, business cards, trade show expenses, brochures, Web site fees, etc.

CAPITAL INVESTMENTS. Your vehicle, expensive painting equipment (sprayers and scaffolding) . . . these items usually depreciate over the years. Use only the depreciation value for that year on your tax forms. Your accountant can help you with this.

UTILITIES. The percentage of heat, gas, lights, water, etc., used in your home exclusively for your business areas can be deducted. Use the same percentage method as described in figuring rent or mortgage deductions.

BANKING. The expense for checks, bank service charges, bad debts, collection costs, etc. used for your business are all deductible.

OFFICE EQUIPMENT EXPENSE. Telephones, supplies, computer, printer, fax, copier, desk, etc., can be deducted *once* . . . the year they were purchased. Ask your accountant about depreciation on expensive office equipment.

INSURANCE. Your business-related insurance fees are deductible.

Variable Expenses

These are expenses that vary with the amount of work you do:

SUPPLIES AND MATERIALS. All paints, brushes, tarps, tape, etc. are deductible.

HIRING HELPERS FOR JOBS. Keep track of their hours and payment.

MILEAGE. Keep records of your miles, gas, and maintenance expenses. If your car is used for both personal and business needs, claim only the amount used for business purposes.

CLOTHING. Any articles of clothing purchased as work clothes are deductible. This includes painter's clothes as well as your "executive" wardrobe used in business presentations.

FEES AND INVOICES FOR BUSINESS PHONE USE, WEB SITES, ETC.

Record Keeping

Keeping records of your business transactions is imperative if you want tax time to go easier on you and be prepared in case of an audit. Your personal and business receipts should be kept separated. Write down your car mileage (31.5 cents per mile is the typical deduction rate used to figure car expenses) and keep receipts for maintenance, etc.

Any of your "listed property" (e.g., cars, computers, cell phones, power tools) can be depreciated, so keep good records of these, including upkeep and repairs.

Paint stores give you a printout of your purchase with the paint's name and formula. File these either with the file of the client for whom you are purchasing the paint, for future orders, or keep all paint records in their own file with the client's name listed somewhere on the order.

Other paint supplies such as brushes, sponges, tarps, ladders, sandpaper, tape, etc., should be kept in a file to make listing their totals under cost of supplies on your tax form easy and dependable. Office supplies, phone records, utility bills, etc., need a place of their own. Keep track of dates on purchases for things that depreciate.

Your Ledger

Record keeping for your income purposes can be a simple ledger or one of the sophisticated software systems available. Quicken is a good one. Either way, you must keep records of your income and outflow. Here's an easy way that can be set up on your computer or logged in a ledger.

With every job, you'll be requesting a half-down deposit. This deposit is to reserve a date for the job to be rendered and to cover material costs and time involved preparing sample boards. At the completion of the job, you'll receive the balance.

Here's where the tricky part comes in. During the course of fulfilling your painting obligations, the client subtracts something or adds something, causing the final balance due to change. Frequently you will be asked to add a hallway now that the client sees how lovely the family room looks. Or . . . the family decides the stencil they originally ordered to go over the dinette window area will now look too gaudy with the ornate faux you just rendered on the walls. I list only the money received on that day, not the total of the job. In case you're interested, in official bookkeeping language this particular practice is called the cash method—because I only record cash that is actually in hand or out of pocket. Therefore, this is how I keep a record of the day's income and expenses:

Daily Accounting Ledger						Week Of:	
	Monday	Tuesday	Wednesday	Thursday	Friday	Saturday	Sunday
Income							
Total							
Expenses							
Rent							
Electricity							
Phone							
Debt Payments							
Advertising							
Freelance							
Maintenance							
Supplies/Office							
Paint Supplies							
Gas							
Other							
Total							
Profit							

Samples of a monthly and a yearly ledger are included in chapter 12 under Useful Forms.

There are wonderful ledgers in the office-supply stores to help you keep professional records, or you can hire a bookkeeper if this area is not one of your strong points.

Client Files

Keeping accurate and up-to-date records of your client transactions is a must. Each client should have his (or her) own file with his name listed at the top. Included in this file should be the proposal and invoice. I use the same form for my proposal and my invoice, as 98 percent of the time I land the job during the first interview. On this form should be the client's name, address, phone (both land and cell), and best time of day to reach them. An itemized account of the job is then listed in the columns requesting price and job description. List the name of the paint selected, which room it's for, and which technique will be rendered—e.g., ragging. List sheen preference: satin or semi. If painting a child's room, list the child's name. Remembering a child's name brings a personal touch to the job, and children love being included in the big decisions concerning their private domains. List equipment requirements (extension ladder, scaffolding, etc.) and any measurements needed to complete the job. If the client is supplying you with a keypad number to their home or a location for a key, write this down.

Any other pertinent information should be listed. Believe me, you will forget things from time to time. You can never take enough notes! List the number of sample boards to be delivered ahead of time to the client and which room they're for.

Finally, write down the client's check number and amount of check under deposit. Write "balance due upon completion" and list that amount. Write the date you are expected to begin. Give the top copy of the two-part or three-part invoice to the client and retain a copy for yourself. The client now has the invoice with the check information for his records. This eliminates the need for receipt books. A sample invoice and client contract is included at the back of the book.

Included in each client file should be any information pertinent to their job. This might include magazine pictures the client gave you to show you a paint technique he admired. Paint chips, fabric samples, and drawings should all be included. If you are entrusted with a client's throw pillow or ceramic tile sample, keep it in a safe place with the customer's name pinned or taped to the item.

Commercial files might include schematic drawings, name of a contractor if there is one also working on the project, and deadline information.

> **TIP:** Always list the paint name and where you bought it! If you are called back for a touch-up, or a client's neighbor saw a room you painted and wants one just like it, you'll have the information at your fingertips. Often patients sitting in a dental office will fall in love with the faux technique you created in the waiting area and request your name. Having the color and technique information readily available looks professional and can assure a speedy bid!

Contracts

I use two kinds of contracts; one for residential and one for commercial. The commercial contract is more involved and covers such issues as bonding and contractor information. Both formats are included at the back of the book. Use these as a guideline. For now, let it suffice to say that being protected and having agreements in writing is important. If a lawsuit should ever ensue over a dispute, a written agreement will make all the difference in the outcome. The sweet woman who offered you homemade cookies a month ago as you sat across from her at her kitchen table could suddenly turn on you if she runs out of money and is unable to pay you after the job is completed. In a desperate effort to save face, or money, she may claim the technique or color was wrong or things were not done according to what she remembers she ordered. Having it all in black-and-white eliminates that problem.

In the contract always stipulate the repercussions if a client requests her deposit back. Again, consult the sample contract at the back of the book. Before you start hyperventilating, thinking this business is fraught with setbacks, let me assure you that in twenty-three years I have never been to court, never sued, and have had a total of three refund requests. I just want you to be covered.

Dealing with Suppliers

You can breathe now. We are moving away from the legalities of your new business and into the mainstream information! Next, under First Things First, we will visit your friendly paint store(s) and set up a commercial account. You will be buying a lot of paint from these people, and you'll want to be on good terms. I have purchased my paint from the same outlet for nineteen years now. I drop by with a pizza or brownies once or twice a year to say "thanks" for the great treatment and prompt service. Paint stores dealing with contractors offer a contractor's discount and, based on the volume of business you do with them, will assign you a discount percentage toward all your purchases; not just paint. Once they get to know you, you'll be able to phone your order ahead of time and it will be waiting for you when you arrive! Nice, huh? The store will provide you with a master palette fan of all their color selections with the colors' names, primer requirements, etc. These palettes are wonderful for selecting colors with the client and matching fabric, tile, or furniture while on site during the interview.

When you order your paint, whether in person or by phone, you will be asked these questions:

1. **"What sheen do you want?"** Here you have five choices: Flat, eggshell, satin, semi-gloss, or gloss. I prefer satin. It gives me the texture I need to render soft, consistent faux finishes and has little shine to it. Avoid flat like the plague! Flat paint has a dry, chalky quality to it and is a nightmare to paint with. This goes for the client's base-coated walls as well; you don't want flat paint for any job.

   The dry finish literally stops your sponge or rag in its tracks and leaves a blotchy look. You may have to ask the client to have the walls painted in a satin finish before you begin if they want a quality faux finish. Adding quality glazing medium to your paint will help, but you will still have a tough time leaving a professional finish. You can tell if it is a flat finish simply by running your hand over the wall. If it feels unduly dry and chalky, it's a flat finish. Contractors use flat paint on homes because it tends to hide flaws or imperfections in the walls. Most homeowners complain about its lack of durability when scrubbing walls to remove fingerprints and grime.

2. **"How much do you want?"** Sometimes a quart of paint is all you'll need for a simple one-room project, such as a color wash. By the time you've added the glazing medium and water, it will cover the job. Some colors cannot be ordered in quarts, and you'll have to buy a gallon. Your paint-store dealer will tell you. Of course, you'll need gallons if you're base-painting the wall in preparation for a multiple finish in faux. I realize ordering paint for your first project may be daunting. How much do you order? It will, of course, depend on the amount of wall you are covering. You can assume one gallon of paint per color for a 10' × 10' room. When the glazing medium, and perhaps water, is added, it goes a long way. You can always order more. If you custom blended a color, make sure when you order the paint that your dealer keeps a record of the recipe! Being off by even a half hue will seriously screw up your finish. If you are ordering from their paint fans, don't count on your memory. Write things down. You can also take the used can with you to order more as most have the recipe listed on a label on the paint lid. As you become more proficient you will get a feel for how much paint to order.

3. **"Interior or exterior?"** Always interior, if you're inside. Occasionally, you'll get an exterior job, and you'll need the appropriate paint. Make sure it's water-based, unless you are rendering an oil-based faux. If in doubt, tell your dealer the nature of the job you're doing, and he'll recommend the best product. If you are fauxing a floor, ask him about the different polyurethane varnishes and epoxies.

4. **"When do you want it?"** Give them some advance notice. Some stores only require a thirty-minute leeway, while others need half a day. Contractors tend to hit the paint stores early in the morning and so avoid trying to place a last-minute order at 7:00 or 7:30 A.M. If you need it early the next morning, call the day before.

TIP: Be careful when ordering paint colors. Double check your order and make sure you give the dealer the correct information. Some paints cannot be returned, and it will become a disadvantage to have you as a customer if you are continually changing orders.

TIP: If your client has already picked a paint color, or her interior designer has recommended a shade provided by a certain paint retailer such as Sherwin Williams or Benjamin Moore, you don't necessarily have to purchase the paint from those stores. Most paint outlets, including the paint department at Home Depot, have all the paint suppliers' codes in their computers and can "pull up" a name and paint code and reproduce the color for you. This saves you from having to set up accounts at several dealerships.

3

HOW TO BUILD YOUR BUSINESS

Finding potential clients in this business is easier than you may think. The fact that faux finishing is big business and is more recognized every year for its beauty and durability means your skills are already in demand. All you need is to do a little footwork and acquire some good people skills. The people skills will be covered in chapter 4; for now, let's concentrate on lining up a support system in the business world.

First, assemble a professional portfolio. This can be a large photo album containing any photographs you've taken of your work, a binder full of sample boards, and a briefcase or carrier bag. If you've spent most of your time practicing sample boards and have few photographs of walls you've actually painted, then you need to improvise a little in this department. Faux-finish a few walls in your own home or get a good friend to let you paint hers. She gets a good deal on beautiful walls, and you acquire some photographs. If you are offering murals and faux finishing, divide your album into two sections, one for each service you're offering. If you're also carrying stencil brushes around and will do regular interior painting, add these sections as well. A few years ago, I began painting room screens when I realized their popularity was making a comeback. I now have a separate area for photographs of these and hand-painted fireplace screens. Decorative furniture, accessories, and calligraphy are also good add-ons.

Keep your sample boards in a professional binder. A section covering sample boards and how to paint them follows in this chapter. These are literally your bread and butter. Not only do they show your talent and range of techniques, they are invaluable in helping clients decide on the spot which color, technique, and sheen they prefer. More jobs are landed in the first interview by pulling out a sample board that makes the client's heart go pitter-patter than by any other strategy. Holding a sample board rendered in a Golden Champagne glaze with a satin base burnished to perfection in an Old World technique behind their burgundy leather couch is going to get shrieks of appreciation. Describing it or showing a magazine picture of the look you're thinking of just doesn't carry the same impact.

Making Professional Contacts

Once you've set up a professional portfolio, and you have your sample boards, business cards, calendar (more about setting up calendars later in this chapter), and invoices, let's see whose door we can knock on.

Interior Decorators

Referrals from interior designers and decorators are a great source of new clientele. These professionals rarely have the time or the desire to paint the walls themselves. If they can give the name of a reputable artist to their clients who want walls painted to go with their newly acquired furnishings and drapes, these interior decorators not only look good but also generally pocket a commission. The standard "kickback" to a designer who has referred you to a client is around 15 percent. I know several designers kind enough to pass my name and card around, and parting with a small portion of my paycheck is fine with me. Your clout rises dramatically when a respected interior decorator recommends you. The burden of selling yourself to the client is greatly reduced. As these decorators see several clients a week, this source of clientele is huge. The moment I receive a half-down deposit, I cut a check for the 15 percent to the designer for the amount of the deposit *only*. I give them the balance when the job is completed and I've received my balance due.

The reason for this is that the job description could change during the course of the project. As mentioned before, things vary sometimes once the job is started. Clients may have a financial emergency arise and decide not to go ahead and have you do the dining room and kitchen as first planned. After looking over the invoice, they may pay you for the work already done in the living room and forgo the rest for now. If you had paid the designer 15 percent of the entire bid, you'd be out money or left with the embarrassing decision of requesting part of it back. Then there's the flip side: the client is so pleased she adds on more rooms and the bid is now double what it originally was. You'd want to compensate the designer accordingly.

> **TIP:** I give a 15 percent commission to designers for the initial job only. Any repeat business I get from that client or referrals from the client to other people becomes my income alone. This is standard in the industry.

Take good care of your designers. There are probably a dozen faux painters vying for their attention. If you treat a client they've referred to you badly, or your work lacks luster, you can be replaced. Cards of gratitude to them and occasional flowers are not a bad idea!

Paint Contractors

Most paint-store outlets will put your cards on their bulletin boards if you ask nicely. Get to know the people behind the counter! They will give your name out to customers who happen to ask, "You don't know any good faux painters, do you?" As I mentioned before, I have used the same paint store to buy my wall paints for nineteen years. I drop by with brownies occasionally and joke with the counter people when I'm in there. I also refer my clients to them for their paint needs, and it is duly noted. I always send a note or make a personal call to thank them for any referrals that come my way due to their kind words.

Other paint contractors are the ones working on new homes or businesses. Very often, you will be on site with interior painters hired to paint the client's walls in a solid color. You have been hired to finish a few rooms in a dramatic faux for visual impact. Working well with painters not only makes your time with them more enjoyable, but they may refer you to clients needing faux work they don't offer.

> **TIP:** You may run into the same painting companies from time to time on new homes, remodels, and commercial jobs. It pays to have a good working relationship with them. Nothing is more miserable than working around someone you've established a derogatory relationship with. By being courteous and making occasional compliments on their quality of work, you insure good future working conditions. More about this in Dealing with Contractors, in chapter 6.

Builders

Early in my career, I was fortunate enough to meet a custom home builder whose reputation in large-scale home building was impeccable. Steve Spanjer with Spanjer Construction began referring me to his clients who wanted faux work and murals painted. This wonderful builder has given me too much work over the years to keep count. To top it off, he has never allowed me to give him any commission on his kind referrals.

If you can hitch your paint cart to a home builder or commercial developer, you will be way ahead in the referral game. These people are always busy and starting one project after another. Make sure your work is always of the highest caliber, and they'll remain loyal to you. If you can send business their way, so much the better. Some builders who specialize in tract homes will use your services for their model homes. Let's take a look at this special area of advertisement:

MODEL HOMES. Builders or interior decorators of model homes are always looking for artists to faux paint the home's walls or render murals, especially children's room murals. You are usually expected to do this gratis, in exchange for the advertising you'll receive. A great number of people go through these models every year and are interested in acquiring the name and phone number of the artist who created such beautiful walls. Your cards are usually left on an entry table or sometimes handed out by the on-site spokesperson. Remember also, when these models close, new ones open. Treat the builder or designer right, and this can be a long-standing career relationship.

> **TIP:** Remember one important thing when dealing with designers, home builders, paint contractors, etc.: the referral program works both ways. Try and return the favor, even if you're giving the professional a commission on the work they're throwing your way. Tell people looking for a great designer or builder that you know just the person who'll do a quality job for them. This type of give-and-take creates a lasting bond that usually blossoms into a lifelong friendship. I treasure these relationships and take special care to preserve them.

Homeowners

Obviously, if you do a "bang-up" job on a client's home, she will sing your praises to everyone who oohs and aahs over her walls. There is no better form of advertisement and obtaining referrals. Later in this chapter is a referral program I offer homeowners, designed to give them a kickback for referring me to their friends.

Restaurants and Other Commercial Sites

If cold-calling doesn't bother you, walking into a commercial site under construction to leave a card and perhaps set up an appointment with the owner is a great way to land jobs.

Sometimes the builder's sign is out front with a phone number. You can call ahead, if you'd rather, and try to obtain the name of the new business's owner and make an appointment that way. Some businesses are franchises and usually have artists they fly around to do all their work. Your best bet are the local ones. Don't limit yourself to restaurants. The number of calls I've gotten from pediatric clinics and dental offices has been phenomenal. All the places people are waiting and can study your work are great sources of income.

MAILING/COPIER OUTLETS. Several have had me paint a children's corner so that parents could take care of their mailing needs unhindered.

VIDEO STORES. Here the franchise rule can be bent a little. I have painted murals in video outlets that were nationwide businesses. These stores tend to have a few blank walls scattered around the store and murals of movie stars or a posh faux finish is always welcome. The project where I took a year's supply of movies in trade for half of the job cemented my fame as mother-of-the-year at our home. Our four sons suddenly saw me in a whole new light!

MEDICAL OFFICES are a huge boon to artists. Not only do they have a labyrinth of treatment rooms outside the waiting area, the number of patients traveling through those rooms on any given day is impressive. They will allow you to leave cards at the receptionist's counter. Remember: medical includes dentists, orthopedists, radiologists, etc. Call ahead and always ask to speak to the person who makes the decisions on the office's décor. It is usually not one of the doctors, but an office manager. Simply say, "Hello, my name is Marjorie Jackson and I would like to talk to you about painting your waiting area in a beautiful faux finish or possibly some murals. I'll come to your office and estimate the job in minutes as well as show you some of my work and an idea of what might look great in the area. This is free of charge and I can work around your schedule."

This may be of interest to you: I just returned from bidding a chiropractic office. They were interested in having the treatment ceilings painted to resemble a sky with clouds. The bid was broken down into two parts: one if the clouds were merely white cumulus clouds, and a different bid if they wanted sunset colors pulled into the clouds. While bidding on the ceilings, I recommended the walls be fauxed in a soft Italian plaster look, to give the room a feeling of being in an open-air villa. They loved it and added three more treatment rooms in the same look.

Have extra business cards handy while you are painting. I recently handed out over 25 cards to parents who asked for them at some pediatric dental offices I was painting.

FURNITURE STORES, especially locally owned stores, don't need to follow any dictates of decorating decorum when choosing a look for their furniture venues.

I'm sure you've noticed how many furniture outlets have room dividers fauxed in beautiful finishes to complement the couch or dining room set in that vignette. Even if they have the sections painted already, trends change, and, if you've impressed them with your portfolio, they'll call you when they need a face-lift.

The children's furniture area could use cute murals as well as painted furniture. Holiday store displays could be fauxed, or a message depicted in a wonderful mural.

Think outside the box when coming up with decorative painting ideas. We have a local furniture store with eleven outlets in Colorado. Their commercials always feature wildlife of some kind while the beautiful furnishings remain center stage. My husband suggested I call the main office and offer to paint wildlife murals at the stores. The owner loved the idea but put his own personal twist on it. Yes. He wanted me to paint wildlife murals but not necessarily on the walls . . . he wanted them painted on his fifty-foot-long semi-truck trailers. We painted eleven trailers with everything from horned owls to coyotes in enamel paint. It is still a thrill to see my grizzly bear I painted fifteen years ago grin as it passes me on the interstate.

Internet Advertising

Few things have impacted the advertising arena as much as the Internet. With a few simple programs, blogs, or Web sites you are able to contact potential customers from around the world. To top it all off, it is very cost-effective, and you decide just how many bells and whistles you want to ring and blow. Many avenues are free. Workshops, message boards, and other online communities are handled elsewhere in this book. This section is dedicated to promoting your business online.

Richard Gerald Lowe Jr. has a wonderful site online called *Internet Promotion*. He lists a few of his pet rules for advertising on the Internet.

Rule Number One: "People use search engines, and to get them to your site you MUST show up in the top 50 or so listings for your keywords in all the major search engines." Nothing else will build traffic faster than getting listed in a search engine.

Rule Number Two: "Concentrate a steady effort on getting your links on other sites. This is an excellent, although very time consuming, way to build steady, permanent increases in traffic. Not only that, but Google (and other search engines) base much of their ranking system on the number and the 'quality' of links to a site."

Rule Number Three: "Start free and stay free unless you've got a very good reason to pay for advertising. There are many, many ways to get free advertising on the Web. I've found very little reason to pay for submission services, e-mail lists, banner exchanges, or anything else to advertise my site." (Richard Gerald Lowe Jr., "Internet Promotion: Advertising On The Internet," *www.webspiner.com*)

Richard Lowe makes an excellent point. Of course these tips require you to research or enlist the help of a Web master or someone with a great deal of computer acumen. Much of the information can be found online by asking questions at Google. Type in the names of other faux painters or muralists and take a look at how they are advertising on the Internet.

If you wish to create your own Web site, which I highly recommend, you will first need a domain name.

1. A **domain name** is the same thing as a URL (Uniform Resource Locator). It is the Web address of a site or page. Mine is

www.rpittmancreations.com. You can make your website as simple or as fancy as you want. You will obviously showcase color photos of your artwork, tell about your company, background, awards (if any), techniques and styles you offer, whether you can travel nationally or globally or prefer to remain in your hometown area, etc. Fancier sites have areas for blogs, message boards, product affiliates, and links to other Web sites that could benefit readers.

2. **E-mail campaigns.** E-mail campaigns have become big business. You can target your audience with specials or new products and techniques with the basic goal of keeping your name on their minds. One very successful campaign has infused my inbox with one-page, full-color e-mails listing new menu items for a local restaurant. The e-mails are highly imaginative and offer color photographs of the food that has me drooling on my keyboard. Every month this restaurant's new menu, specials, and gratis recipes pop up as I peruse my e-mails. I began frequenting this venue and I have complimented the owner often on how creative and effective his e-mail campaigns are. You can try to get e-mail addresses from interior decorators for their clientele. Homebuilders and paint stores are great sources, as well as daycares if you are promoting children's murals, home centers, local mailing list stores, and many, many more. Obviously, you will want to build your own clientele by dealing with customers face to face and with those who find your Web site. Most Web sites offer a "Contact Me" section so that visitors can type in their names, e-mail addresses, etc. and ask about your services.

3. **Newsletters.** When a potential customer shows up at your site, they can request your newsletter. These usually go out monthly and are huge promotional tools for your business. As with the e-mails you can list specials, new ideas, and showcase your latest creations.

4. **Free content.** Richard Gerard Lowe, Jr., in his article entitled "Internet Promotion," relays the following information concerning free content:

> "You want to build a steady flow of traffic that puts search engines to shame? Give away content. Some Webmasters create Web graphics, which you can use at will for a return link. Others (like myself)

write articles that anyone can put on their site as long as the signature is included. Some even have little java applets or other doodads which, again, can be included for a link. The massive advantage of this type of promotion is you don't have to link back. They have to link to you, but you don't have to link to them. Thus, there is no PR (Google) risk at all, and you don't have to mess with those awful links pages that no one ever looks at."

5. **Banners.** Banners are those annoying things that flash across the top of your screen when you are searching for information. I have yet to meet anyone who benefited from them. They are so prevalent that most Internet users have come to ignore them. If you feel you want to try them, shop carefully as the price range varies and they will try and sell you the TURBO charged banners that you really don't need.

6. **eBooks** are great if you want to write your own electronic book. These are available for download and distribution by anyone wanting your information. Make sure your links to your sites are prominently displayed. This could result in massive hits to your site if you have created a quality product.

7. **Directories.** Yahoo and DMOZ (Google uses these two directories for its own index) are two free directories. List your site in as many directories as possible.

8. **Minor search engines** can be approached with an automated submission technique. Try and list your link in as many as possible. Go easy on multiple submissions or you could get flagged as a spammer.

9. **Awards.** You can apply for award programs online. The bigger ones will generate a great deal of traffic. You can look into this option by searching "So You Want To Run An Awards Program?" on your search engine.

10. **Press releases.** If you can get yourself listed in a major newspaper or Web site, you could see your traffic skyrocket. These releases can be expensive but are well worth looking into.

11. **Contests.** Some businesses offer contests on their Web sites and have been very successful in creating a great deal of traffic. Perhaps you could feature a "Create Your Own Faux Painting Technique" contest and award the winning recipe with a specialty faux painting

tool, glazing medium, or other related prize, and then feature their technique along with a color photograph on your site.

12. **Message boards, newsgroups, and forums.** Posting updates and breaking news on message boards, newsgroups, and forums will increase traffic to your site. By including your URL address in your signature, you will have people checking out your site to learn more about the person who just posted such insightful information.

13. **Blogs.** This is a great way to promote your site. You can write editorials and articles referencing your site.

14. **Affiliate programs.** Perhaps you are a stenciler and have designed your own stencil template. You can sell your own products on an affiliate program which could lead to links to your Web site posted by other sites promoting your product.

15. **Autoresponses.** By adding an autoresponse to your Web site, you can immediately acknowledge anyone who visits your site with an e-mail thanking them for stopping by.

These are just a few of the helpful promotional tools the Internet offers. There are many books out there, including the popular Dummies series, that can walk you through the art of creating an effective Web site and promoting it to the hilt. At the very least, you have a professional place to send your clients where they can see your work, learn about your ethics and history, and get your contact information. You will also be visible to anyone who types the keyword "murals" into the search engines. Who knows, you may end up in Italy!

Other Ways to Advertise

We've covered the benefit of distributing flyers, contacting designers, and builders, Yellow Pages ads, vehicle lettering, etc. Does this mean we're through with ideas for creative ways to advertise your new venture? Do artists ever run out of ideas? I don't think so either . . . so here are a few more.

Referrals

Tell everyone you know you're in business! More referrals than you can imagine come from someone telling someone else about you. Pass out those cards you just had printed.

Cold Calls

Cold calling has landed me some amazing jobs. We touched on this earlier, but let me give you an example. I usually drive around my city and surrounding areas once a month and look for signs saying "Coming Soon" or new construction signs announcing an upcoming restaurant, medical clinic, etc. I have been very fortunate in the number of bids landed with restaurants, car dealerships, hospitals, retail outlets—the Big Guys!

Several years ago, I noticed a huge building going up and found out it was a local car dealership opening their second outlet. I called and got hold of the owner and simply said, "Hi. My name is Rebecca Pittman and I own Wonderland Productions here in town. I've been doing murals for businesses and homes here for the past twenty years and would love to talk to you about painting something unique for your new dealership. What would you think about a backdrop depicting cars from Henry Ford to present day?" (They are a Ford dealership, which helps!) There was a pause on the other end and just when I thought he'd hung up on me, he said, "Actually we were planning on having some murals done in a food court area we're building in the center of the store. We also have a children's play area we'll need something done with. Let me give you the name of the designer we're working with and you two come up with something."

The food court ended up being 36' × 30' × 15' high and we painted the entire thing to look like you were sitting in Europe looking at the shops. We even painted the floor in faux cobblestone. The children's area ended up depicting dinosaurs driving monster Ford trucks. It was a huge project. I put up a bronze plaque with my name and phone number on it at the entrance to the mural.

The only glitch in the entire project was when one of the owners asked me to please turn off my CD player. Surprised, because the construction workers and I had been listening to music the entire month we were there, I bent over and turned it off.

It was then I realized the reason for the request . . . the music coming from the speakers was Bob Seger's "Like a Rock," which happened to be the new theme song for Chevy!

Some businesses love to do projects in trade. If you're in a local restaurant and feel the walls lack a little luster, approach the owner and tell him what you do for a living. Throw out some quick ideas, a ballpark figure, and say, "If you'd like, we can do part of it in trade." I don't offer the full bid price in trade because the cost of my materials should be covered first.

A huge resource for cold-calling work is children's daycare centers. I approached one of the local members of a large franchise in my town and ended up doing twenty-three of their schools across Colorado. Schools and daycares always want murals and fauxed walls.

New Businesses

Go to the Builder's Exchange and request new information on all new businesses going into your city. They have all the names of new ventures preparing to build and open. Check with places like landscaping companies who receive periodicals of new businesses coming into your community. One here is called the Dodge Report and lists all the new businesses, schools, hotels, etc., scheduling development and requesting bids for exterior and interior work. Getting to companies before they break ground is a huge advantage as they usually budget for all expenses in their start-up proposals.

Print Ads

Frankly, newspaper and magazine ads are a waste of money. They're expensive and generate very little business. If you decide to give this area of trade a try anyway, your best bet, for newspapers, is to list your business under a section entitled "Services." It's usually found in the classifieds section of your paper and is divided into categories of the different service-oriented businesses. If you can afford the expense, you might look into a box ad similar to the ones we discussed when we talked about Yellow Page ads. Place it in the entertainment section if you can; somewhere people spend some time, like when they are checking out movies and restaurant ads.

Local magazines and publications are good sources for trade work. Ask publishers if they'd like their homes or businesses done in trade for ad space.

Organizations

Joining organizations in your community is an incredible way to network and gain leads. Many tradeoffs are done here; it's the "you scratch my back and I'll scratch yours" philosophy. Take along plenty of business cards. Your local Chamber of Commerce has listings it'll mail to you of all the organizations meeting in your community.

It would also be a good idea to join professional groups. You can find the following faux painting organizations on the Internet by typing their names, as listed below, into a search engine:

- **PDCA** Painting and Decorating Contractors of America was established to help regulate and improve standards and working conditions in the painting industry. Their Web site is *www.pdca.org.*
- **The Portal to Our Faux Painting World** includes an international directory of decorative painters, faux painting classes, message center, chat room, e-mail group, faux finishing shop for all your supply needs, and a classifieds section to run your own ad.
- **Bozzle.com** lets you advertise your business online for as little as $15 a year.
- **Pro Faux** offers a What's New Gallery, showcasing the latest faux techniques, workshops, products, and free booklets.
- **PDRA** Organization offers *The Faux Finisher Magazine* and much more.
- **Stencil Artisans League, Incorporated (SALI)** was organized in 1983 and is dedicated to promoting and preserving the art of stenciling and decorative painting, including faux finishes, plasters, concrete products, murals, and other forms of artistic painting.

Opportunities for artistic and professional growth through education, certification, public awareness, and networking are just a few
of the benefits of membership in this organization. Their Web site
is *www.sali.org*.

- **Society of Decorative Painters (SDP)** is a great resource for all
aspects of decorative painting. Their focus includes fine detailing for
muralists interested in taking their craft to a higher level. They have
many talented teachers who specialize in details such as wildlife elements, flowers, etc. The Web site is *www.decorativepainters.org*.

The last time I checked, 81,000 sites popped up when I typed "Faux
Painting" into my browser's search engine. Most advertise workshops
worldwide teaching faux painting techniques; however, there are many organizations to be found as well. The above listings are the ones I feel offer the
most to the beginning faux painter—as well as allowing you to interface with
other artists like yourself. Several provide the opportunity to advertise your
new business and acquaint you with the latest tools, techniques, books, and
videos. Happy surfing!

For local organizations, call your local chamber of commerce and ask for
listings of groups meeting in your area.

Networking

The obvious way to start networking is talking to family and friends.
Extending your networking out into the community could involve letting
church members know you have started a new business. Carry cards with
you to your children's sporting events, plays, daycare meetings, parent-
teacher conferences, school open houses, and fundraising events. Become
involved in local clubs and organizations that appeal to you, whether related
to decorative painting or not. You will find people wanting your services in
every branch of life. I have a friend who joined a local Toastmasters group
and landed several lucrative painting jobs from members. Attend library
functions, rec center seminars, workshops, and expos and always have your
cards ready.

Contact your Chamber of Commerce to ask about local groups that
might interest you. You can also find this information online on your

Chamber of Commerce's Web site. The listings of all the organizations in your area will be available, along with when they meet, membership requirements, etc. This is a great way to expand your horizons and make new contacts.

Volunteer to be on committees for charity work or donate a mural or faux finish to a worthy cause. Not only will your work be on display, but often there is also a favorable blurb placed in the local paper about charity work. Your creation could be on the front page of your newspaper, and people love to support those who give back to the community.

Ask architects, interior designers, and home builders what organizations they support or are involved in. The National Association of Home Builders can lead you in the right direction as well.

Join the professional organizations listed above. Networking on a national level allows you to learn new fads in the industry and to ask for questions, as well as share information, you might have been hesitant to in your hometown due to competition factors. You can never learn enough about your chosen craft. Meeting with people who share your passion also keeps your flame of enthusiasm alive and gives you that "Let's take it to the next level!" feeling.

Obviously, with the far-reaching impact of the computer world, global networking is now at our fingertips. It is the easiest way to reach thousands of potential customers. There are thousands of decorative painting Web sites and forums utilizing information from artists around the world. You can blog, Twitter, e-mail, live chat, and message board your way across the continent in these informative forums. My good friend Martin Allen Hirsch's Web site, MuralsPlus, offers quick answers to business, faux, and mural questions. FauxTalk and Atrium Online are two other Web sites to check out. The potential to learn and network globally is immense. We are so blessed to have all this information at our fingertips.

- FauxTalk, *www.fauxstuffonline.com/FauxTalk/*
- MuralsPlus, *www.MuralsPlus.com*
- Atrium Online, *www.atriumonline.org*
- The Faux Finish School, *www.faux-painting-finishing-board.com*
- The FinishingSource, Inc. *www.fauxfinishingsource.com/forum*

Upcoming Events

Watch your local newspapers for upcoming events and new stores.

Country Clubs

Country clubs are great sources for faux work when old colors become tired. As many now offer their rooms for weddings, portable painted panels such as room screens would make beautiful backdrops for special events. A local country club had me bid on room dividers with a faux finish on one side and painted topiary trees on the other. Again . . . think outside the box!

Child's Play

We talked a little about children's play areas. Do you realize how many different types of stores are now offering a section for children to play to encourage parents to shop longer? I was recently in a name-brand appliance center shopping for a new dryer, and they had a wonderful children's area complete with television. Stores offering copier services, where customers are typically there for a while, are great places to contact with your proven "Excuse me, but I have an idea for you!" format. Laundromats, cleaners, banks, video stores, etc.—you get the idea.

Animal Habitats

If you're into murals, try pet stores, veterinarians, and clinics dealing with animals. They use just as many murals as daycare centers. There is a danger of coming home from one of these jobs with more than just a paycheck, but if your spouse or roommate doesn't mind the new litter box and a little cat hair, you should be all right.

Think Creative!

Everywhere you go are opportunities. Don't overlook white columns in front of banks and malls. Wouldn't a lovely marbling be gorgeous? Just remember, don't push. A "just thought I'd mention it to you" touch is perfect when approaching a prospective client.

This should leave you with no excuse that you lack avenues to pursue in your quest for drumming up clientele. You no doubt have innovative ideas of your own. Don't be nervous about approaching people. I've discovered that, seven times out of ten, they are thinking about doing something to spruce the place up; they just don't know what to do. A number of cold-calls were impressed with my ideas to make their businesses more efficient by adding children's areas, etc. Go in with a caring attitude and *listen* to their ideas. Show an interest in their business and ask how long they've been there and how the location is working out for them. There is no substitute for genuinely caring about the clients and wanting to see them succeed or have the home or business of their dreams.

Building Your Portfolio

Purchase a nice briefcase or leather carrying case to hold your calendar, cards, color sample fan, magazine pictures, faux books, invoices, calculator, etc. Pack a few pens; they tend to get left behind at the clients (ahem!). I've used the same leather carrying case for ten years. It is weathered and shows character. It has compartments for pens, cards, and larger areas for books, invoices, etc. The shoulder strap frees my hands to lug in the sample board folder and my photo album.

When putting together your presentation trio (briefcase, sample folder, and photo album), keep things organized. Taking five minutes of the client's time while you dig through your bag for a magazine clipping you've got somewhere that shows the exact look they're thinking of for their kitchen is tiresome. Going through your bag periodically to reacquaint yourself with its contents is beneficial. Mine tends to load up pretty fast with information and notes, clippings, and clients' fabric samples.

Here's a checklist for your briefcase or bag: calculator, invoices/proposals, business cards, notepad and pens, Day-Timer or calendar, a few books illustrating the different kinds of faux finishes offered. This helps narrow the client's focus and saves time. Now you can offer the appropriate sample boards. These books also show the benefit of painted walls when displayed with whole-room furnishings. Many of your clients are not "visual," and seeing a picture, whether from a book or one of your photos, helps immensely in conveying your point concerning the benefit of color. They also can see that, contrary to popular belief, color does not always make a room look smaller but rather enhances it!

This pertains to mural bids as well. I have an entire crate of mural books in my car that travels with me. They include wildlife, European art, the old masters, seascapes, floral, wall borders, whimsy, and children's areas, to name a few. Again, many clients know they want something wonderful on their walls, they just don't know what. Showing them something that makes their face break out in a smile greatly progresses the meeting. You will also see the ones that bring a turned-up nose so you'll know to avoid those themes.

Carry envelopes to hold paint chips, fabric swatches, pictures, or any other small items your client might hand you to facilitate their project. Write the client's name and phone number on the envelope and its contents. Take extra good care of any property entrusted to you.

Contents of Your Photo Album

Your album obviously contains pictures of your work. You can purchase a regular photo album with plastic pages divided into photo-size sections or invest in one with a single-page format where you adhere your photos to the page. I recommend the pages with individual inserts, as clients will pull your pictures in and out and sometimes ask to keep one overnight to show a spouse.

Keep your photos updated and always bring a camera to your job sites.

My photo album is divided into categories: commercial and residential. The residential is further broken down into room descriptions: kitchen, living room, etc., with a separate section for children's rooms that can also be shown to commercial clients wanting a toddlers' area. If you have panoramic photos and can't find an album with sections large enough to hold them, improvise by adhering a sturdy pocket to the inside back cover. A cut-up manila folder works well.

Your Sample Board Binder

The large portfolios offered at art-supply stores work for sample boards. They have ample space and handles. As I said earlier, anything with handles will make your life easier; we lug around a lot of stuff! The section on preparing sample boards follows, but for now make sure you purchase a binder that will accommodate at least a 2' × 2' sample board. If your inventory of boards is ponderous, try and pare them down by finding out from the client ahead of time what look they're interested in and for which room. Yes, you will probably get an "I have no idea . . . I'm relying on you to recommend something!" response, but it's worth a shot. If you've made extensive samples, try offering a sampling of the different finishes in the binder you carry into the house or business and, once the clients have focused on a technique they like, bring in the boards representing that color or technique from your car. Many interior decorators start out with an overview of mini-blinds, for instance, and then retrieve the desired look from the van. Just keep boards organized to avoid wasted time. Having them separated into categories, such as ragging, plaster, sponged, chamois, etc., will speed things along. Sometimes the client is more interested in color selection, so it pays to render your boards in a variety of colors *and* techniques. Very often, you'll hear, "I like the Old World look in the color wash but I like the color you have over here in the ragging."

Setting Up Your Calendar

Select a good two-to-three-year diary or portable calendar to carry in your briefcase or carrier. As you set up a date with a client to begin their project, block out the number of days you anticipate needing for that job. I usually write the name of the client and draw a line through the next few days with brackets on each end noting the start and end of their project.

Now, here's the important part. Plan at least two days between projects! For one, you'll need the time to recharge your batteries if it's been a long project laden with ladders and obstacles. Two, this allows you some space should the project go over or the client adds a hallway, etc. Having another project breathing down your neck is stressful.

Decorative painting, whether in the faux arena or murals and stencils, is tiring, both mentally and physically. You will be using muscles you don't normally use. Give yourself some space to regroup and energize! Any creative process is a mental process, and you need to be fresh for each job in order to bring your best to the table.

Be sure to pencil into your calendar any family events, holidays, school days off, and any other reason you would not be able to book that day. I don't know about your area, but here in Colorado the kids get quite a few days off for teacher conferences and other scheduled meetings. If children don't factor into your scheduling, then skip this part. If they do, and you prefer to be home, check the school calendars that come home with them the first day of school and block the no-attendance days off on your calendar now. Calling clients to say, "Oops," should be avoided as much as possible. Decide how many days you're taking for Thanksgiving and Christmas and draw a line through those days.

Pencil onto your calendar any deadlines for samples, paint pick-up, etc. If you are due to deliver five sample boards to Mrs. Parsons on Saturday of this week, write it down—along with the time and address, if there's room. I love having all the information in one small, compact location. If you told the paint dealership you'd pick up a gallon of paint on Friday afternoon, pencil it in—along with the color of the paint, if you'd like. If there's a section for phone numbers on your calendar, or a Notes section, write down the names, phone numbers, and addresses of all the clients you'll be dealing with in that month, along with vendors you typically call, such as paint stores. You'll make a lot of calls in this job, and it's nice to have all the information at your fingertips.

With today's technology, a lot of people are keeping this kind of information on their computers, cell phones and Blackberries, which is fine. I am a little old-fashioned in that I like to have it on a paper calendar that I can take out, scribble on, figure out the next few months of work and play. I carry it with me everywhere and the great part is it never goes into a "no service" area, loses power, or shuts down due to a dead battery. There is nothing wrong with using both. Computers and Blackberries will even alert you to a meeting, conference calls, and other appointments for those of us with "selective memories."

Keep a bottle of white-out handy. You will get postponements, cancellations, and "bump-ups" occasionally. Construction delays on new homes and businesses is a given. Don't ever etch in stone a date given to you by a construction team to begin your project. This is nothing against these companies, it's just that delays in building are part of the package. Pencil in the date they tell you they'll be finished and out of your way. Then check with them regularly to see if they're on track. Tell any clients you have booked on either side of a new construction project that there may be a small change in dates if the project you've already booked for a new home or business runs into delays or, *gasp*, finishes early. I am in the middle of one of those right now, and the

61

date has changed four times. The clients you have booked after the new construction job are usually thrilled that, due to delays, you can bump them up to a little earlier than you thought. It usually balances out; just be flexible and don't sweat the "sawdust"!

Someone may call you and say, "I'm sorry, but we won't be able to keep the date we scheduled with you. My husband booked a cruise to surprise me, not knowing I had set aside these dates for you to paint. Could you please move me into your next available time slot?" Assure her that a chance to snorkel in Jamaica tops having her walls glazed in tangerine, and politely tell her your next open date. Remind her that the down payment now anchors the new date, and you will be turning other clients down for that time slot. Ask if she's *sure* that date works for her. There is a section in the sample contract at the back of the book covering what happens if someone cancels and wants a refund.

Always keep your calendar in one place or return it to your carrier after you're through with it. Loosing this valuable tool is a major headache. (No, this one has *not* happened to me . . . yet!)

Sample Boards

Making sample boards is time-consuming and may seem like a lot of wasted time, but, believe me, the time it will save you in redoing a wall the client decides is not what they want, makes it well worth it. The groundwork you do ahead of time will pay off in several ways:

1. You have selected the color that will work with everything in the room. You know this because you've held it up to the wood trim, fabrics, floor, etc. The client has initialed it and is happy. The client has taped it to the wall in the room you're doing and has lived with it overnight to see it in different lighting situations.
2. You are more confident going in, because you have already done the faux process on the sample, recorded your steps and color mixtures, and know it will look great.
3. After doing the sample board in the color and technique you will be using on the wall, you have a good idea how long it is going to take you to paint the wall(s) and you can plan the day accordingly.

Always make sure the technique you are rendering on a sample board can be duplicated on a wall. Don't do an elaborate sample board just to get the job, knowing you can't possibly do all those steps on a wall and make a profit. If the client wants a process requiring eight times around the room to render it, charge accordingly. You are literally painting the same wall, consuming the same amount of time, for each glaze.

Another reason for assuring your sample is exactly the technique and color you intend to use on the wall is that the client will hold the sample up to the completed wall and compare. This happens a lot. Don't switch colors on them after they've initialed a board (more about this later) just because you have an extra gallon of Golden Wheat in the garage and it's *pretty* close to the Harvest Wheat they ordered!

Record Your Samples

Have a notebook specifically for recording sample board information. This book keeps track of your clients and their samples. Write the name of the client on the back of each sample board and the colors used. In your notebook, do the same, but also add next to the paint whether it was satin, eggshell, semigloss, or gloss. (We ignore flat paint in this business!) Did you paint the wall in the paint's true color or was it tinted with white or shaded with black? If so, in what quantities were the other hues added? What tool was used? (Sponge, rag, comb, etc.) How was it used? (Dragged, swiped, padded?) Did you use a primer or finish coat? How long did the sample take you? What texture is the wall you're painting on? (Flat, orange-peel, or knockdown?) Record it in a notebook with numbers corresponding to the boards. Putting a small drop of the paint colors you are using on your notes makes an easy reference. I use index cards for this information and keep it in the client's file. Now you have precise notes in case the client needs a touch-up or likes the wall so much that she has you back later to do another room the same way. There's also the client who saw a wall you did in someone else's house and wants the same thing done. This is a must for the professional decorator. Keep notes.

Charging for Sample Boards

I don't charge for sample boards unless they pass a certain criteria. I tell the client they are included in the deposit price if I am awarded the job. If the client wants to see a sample in order to decide if she wants to give you the job or not, then charge a small fee for your time, stipulating that, if you get the job, the fee will come out of the bill. The sample boards remain the property of the painter, and this should be mentioned. If the client keeps asking for more boards, charge a fee, stating that the first three boards are included in the bid, after three there is a charge of $20 per board.

Have the clients initial the back of their sample board as soon as they agree on one. This is a safety net for you. They can't come back and say the wall is not what they were expecting if you hold the board they okayed up to the wall and it matches exactly.

> **TIP:** If you would like to show the boards to other clients as part of your portfolio, and having another client's name and signature on the back makes the board look used, then tell your new client that this is a sample of a technique and color that have been very popular for you and would work well with their colors as well. This helps focus the client and saves time for you. You may have to do a whole new board, or have them sign the same one. Using an index card taped to the back that the client signs off on, or anything that can be removed, poses a problem. They can bring up the point that the card could have been removed and switched when they said they were unhappy with the finished project. It is still better to have them sign directly onto the back of the board.

Sample Board Preparation

Your sample boards should be made from artist's mat boards or a sturdy illustration board. These can be found at any art supply or craft store. A recent discovery I made was at Home Depot—they now carry packages of sample practice boards. For the cost of $1.69 (at the time of this printing), you receive four boards in a good sturdy stock. The more sturdy stock such as an artist's mat board remains flat when wet instead of curling up and warping like poster board. If you are rendering a stencil for a long-running border design, you can purchase blank-stock wallpaper from your local home center. It can be unrolled to any length for a stencil design so your client can get a good idea of how the running border will look surrounding her kitchen. Again, the more samples you render, the more your portfolio grows. Always keep your samples! These remain your property after a project is completed!

If you are offering a sample of a mural, the above stock will do nicely. You can also purchase a sturdy watercolor artist's pad and do a simple wash of color over your sketch. My portfolio pictures usually suffice to show my painting style, degree of detail, etc., but you will often be asked to do a quick sketch of the mural. You'll read more about mural samples and bidding in chapter 9.

Painting furniture and moldings require samples to be done on wood chips. You can get unfinished pine and other woods at your local home center and coat them in the requested stain, antiquing glaze, paint, or decorative trim.

If you want a larger background to display a painting sample, whether faux or mural work, you can get sailcloth, cambric cloth, vinyl banners, and other materials which can be rolled up and carried or shipped. Your local sign company carries a multitude of materials that can be rendered upon with everything from metal, vinyl, and Coroplast to Plexiglas, Lexan, and banner paper. You will often be asked to paint unusual things in this business, such as boats, campers, metal garage doors, even Plexiglas or air-blasted signs. Knowing where to go for necessary materials is always helpful.

Some artists laminate their sample boards to protect them from dirt and constant handling. You can purchase styrene plastic for your projects if you want a totally indestructible board. Practice will dictate which surfaces work best for you and your clients.

I would like to offer one word of warning here—I realize the popular method for painting large sample boards is to tape off a one-inch border around the board to accommodate handling. The down-side to this is that the color does not run all the way to the edge of the board and when holding it up to a client's wall for reference, or next to a fabric for comparison, the white one-inch area is distracting and takes away from the flow of your sample onto the wall or fabric.

Coat your boards with the same base coat color you will be using in the project. Colors react differently when painted onto various hues. What may look great on a white background could take on undertones and look too dark or too light on a colored base coat already in existence. You can tape off an upper corner of the board after you've painted the base and before you start the faux or mural sample, allowing you and the client to see what the base color is or will be before the techniques are applied. Painting the base first not only gives you a surface similar to what you'll actually be painting on, but it discourages the boards from rolling up when they become damp from the glaze. If the boards do curl, lay them face down after they're dry and place heavy books on their backs; they'll straighten out.

A good size sample board is 2' × 2'. Many workshops today have their students create large samples in the 3' × 2' range. Make them at least large enough to give the client a good idea of what the new surface will look like and a vantage point to compare couch material, drapes, and wood trim. Remember to record all steps and colors on the back and in your notebook as you go. Memory cannot be trusted when multiple colors are thrown into the mix.

> **TIP:** While it may seem smart to record your color recipe, color swabs, steps, and notes right on the back of the sample to keep it simple, it allows others to copy your technique and color selection if they retain your samples for consideration. If they are shopping your competition, you don't want them having your exact recipe and then underbidding your estimate to land the job.

If you are doing a sample for something other than a wall, like a cabinet face, molding, trim, etc., try and get a replica of the piece at a home builder's store. Sand, prime, and paint the new piece to show how the finished product will look.

Keep your sample boards in their binder when not showing them to the client. Don't leave them tossed in the car or cluttering the garage. You worked hard on these, and you don't want them dog-eared and bent.

Showing the Client the Boards

When bidding on a job, show the client no more than three boards at a time. Most people become overwhelmed with too many decisions, and it could cost you the job if they suddenly "shut down" and say, "I just can't decide. Maybe I should think about it."

I've had clients get nervous on me when I've tried to whittle down their choices to a few color selections. Some people panic over decision making. That's why they called you; to sweep in riding your white van and flourishing your sample boards with *exactly* the technique and color they would have chosen. The trick is to make the client feel as though she did know what she wanted, she just needed you to show it to her.

If the client is not happy with one of the three samples you brought in, take it away and bring in another one, but try to have only three on the table at one time. If her confusion continues, try this: "You know you don't have to be happy with the technique *and* the color on a particular sample board. Perhaps you like the ragging technique on this board (point to one) but would rather have it done in the color on the sponged board (point to that one). Let's do this . . . let's start with the technique you like the best. What draws your eye and pleases you more? The broken plaster look or the sponged? Do you like the smooth feel of the Venetian plaster or the rough finish of a skip-troweled look?"

Now, give her a minute and don't interrupt. Let her take a good long look. While she's doing this, take a good look at the walls in her home. What finish are they? Knockdown, orange-peel, flat? If the client is still indecisive, you can gently add, "I notice your walls are a heavy knockdown texture. The sponged Old World glazes look particularly gorgeous on this type of texture. The deep pits add their own hint of shadow and depth." If the wall is flat, "Ragged techniques or broken plaster really show up well on flat walls because their smooth surface enhances the pattern created by the rag or trowel."

Hopefully, you now have her narrowed down to the technique. Now take some of the different colored boards over and hold them behind the couch or put them up to the dining room drapes. This will usually show the client immediately how one color plays off another. If she says the green looks nice, but maybe a little lighter would be better, grab the trusty color sample fan you obtained from the paint store and show her a sampling of greens in a lighter shade. If she chooses one or more colors she'd like to see in the green using the ragged look you've recommended, you're on your way. Write down on her invoice and in your notepad the names of the paint chips she selected and the paint store the fan is from. Tell her when to expect the boards and end with something positive and upbeat, "Don't worry. If these boards don't work, we'll just keep doing them until we get you happy! I offer three free sample boards included in my bid, and if we need more than that, the cost is minimal. This is going to look beautiful. You did a great job picking out colors and techniques! There's a lot to choose from!" (More on dealing with the client is coming up in chapter 4.)

The Referral Program

I'd like to end this chapter by adding a little program that has served me well. Whenever I am with a client and she shows enthusiasm about my portfolio and photos, I tell her, "Well, if you tell your neighbors or friends about me and they call for an appointment, make sure they mention your name so I can give you credit. I'll give you 10 percent of whatever their order comes to, to go toward a future project of yours. It's my way of saying 'thank you,' as referrals are the reason I no longer require a Yellow Page ad. I appreciate the nice words and your time to tell others about me."

There will be numerous times when the client you're seeing wishes she could have you paint more rooms, but she just can't afford it right now. Having a way to gather some credit simply by telling a few friends makes her very excited. Do not let her put a referral credit toward the balance she will owe you on the present job. If the new referral suddenly changes her mind before you begin the project, whether canceling or reducing the amount of work they originally wanted, you have now lost money by reducing your bill to the client who referred you. Make all credit for future projects, after the new referral's project is completed and the bill paid.

This program has several benefits: 1) Most other painters don't offer it, so that's just one more good reason to hire you and not someone else. 2) The 10 percent you'll give her is a drop in the bucket when compared to the new job(s) you'll be bidding on, thanks to her kind referral. Referrals snowball . . . in a hurry. Make sure your gratitude is genuine. I sincerely appreciate these referred jobs and take pride in the fact that someone liked me and my work well enough to spread the word. A thank-you note highlighting the amount of credit the client has earned is a great touch. If the referral comes after you've finished the job and moved on, try this: I usually send a gift certificate to a nice restaurant or bookstore as a way of showing my gratitude. It never ceases to amaze me how thrilled and surprised people are at this kind gesture. It's all good business and a wonderful way to tell your clients you appreciate them!

4

LET'S GO SEE THE CLIENT!

Although the usual dress code of an interior painter is paint-splattered clothes (and you'll have plenty of those!), you will also need a professional wardrobe to conduct interviews and attend business meetings.

Dressing for Success

If you're a woman and prefer slacks and a nice blouse rather than a dress, that's fine. The key here is to look like a business owner with taste.

Leave the clunky jewelry and worn sandals for the neighborhood barbecue. Gentlemen, resist the urge to show off those amazing biceps with a tank top, and sport a nice shirt and slacks instead. A tie is a nice touch, especially if it's a commercial bid. You are in a very visual business and are therefore able to bend a few fashion rules. Your clients actually expect a little "color" when dealing with artists and interior decorators. I've seen some decorators go to the extreme, however, and it becomes comical rather than attractive. Find a subtle balance.

If you want to dress up a pair of Levi's and a dress shirt, add a blazer. This goes for women and men. It's a very trendy look and adds a layered appeal that always seems a little more dressy. A tailored look is what you're going for. Don't wear your Sunday best; just take care to look nice.

A word here about the condition of your clothes: always make sure you're pressed and polished. Shoes often get overlooked, so take a minute and make sure they are clean. Wear a nice pair of socks (holes-free) in case you are asked to remove your shoes at a client's house. This is happening more and more as it becomes acceptable and even expected to be asked to shed your shoes when nice white carpets are involved.

Watch the cologne and perfume. I had a young man come to interview with me for a job as a freelance muralist, and the amount of cologne he had on just about bowled me over. I couldn't concentrate on his portfolio because I was getting a serious buzz from whatever he was wearing. Here's the rule of thumb for perfumes and colognes: always put them on twenty minutes before a planned meeting to allow them to "diffuse" a little; "less is more" really applies here.

Keep the makeup subtle and the hairstyles polished. The old image of the New York artist living in holey jeans with hair to his waistline is outdated. A professional haircut gives a successful appearance, and you'll be taken more seriously because of it. Women, if you have long nails (and if you do *and* you paint, I want your recipe!) keep them manicured and shortened. Talons just don't work with sponges and taping off trim work. Men need to keep their nails clean and well tended as well. Dirty nails are a turn-off, and claiming you're an artist and can't help it doesn't cut it.

Hygiene is very important when dealing with the public, especially in the privacy of their homes. You may think a focus on this is childish; after all, you're grown people wanting to begin your own business. Let me tell you something. Unfortunately, I have worked around a number of grown people who owned their own businesses, and I had to move downwind of them! It's amazing—but true.

Now, you look professional, smell great, and you could go from this interview to model for a spread in *GQ* without even changing socks! Great! One last thing . . .

Smile big! Your personality will win you this bid every bit as much as your superior talent. If you're having a bad day, leave the mood at home and go out the door with a smile on your face. Trust me! This is one area you can't ignore.

Your Briefcase

We've already covered your briefcase or carrier, as far as its contents are concerned. Make sure its *exterior* looks just as sharp as you do. Don't go to see a prospective client with a worn-out briefcase held together with cord or covered with paint spatters. Every part of your presentation will be analyzed, either consciously or subconsciously, and the client will make a mental note of your professional persona.

When you are in the client's home, ask if you can set your briefcase down in a certain area. Clients may not want it on the floor due to curious pets, and they may be extremely sensitive to things being set on their highly polished table. Just say, "Is it all right if I set this here?" If you do put it on a table, never drag it toward you if it has metal tabs. Don't remove pens, pencils, paper clips, or other small items and leave them lying around if the client has small children.

> TIP: Take along a pad or coloring book and crayons to keep little ones busy while you talk to mom or dad. Any time a parent receives company, the child wants in on it and will interrupt you repeatedly. If you want a leg up on landing a bid, take along diversions. But always ask before you hand children anything.

A few weeks ago, I was giving a bid to a woman in a nine-thousand-square-foot home. Her personality was, quite frankly, condescending and rude. I kept the smile on my face and tried to treat her as I do all my interviews. For thirty minutes she complained about the other artists who had come to bid on jobs for everything from outdoor stucco work to retiling her kitchen. I was regaled with stories of poor conduct and tardiness. Just when I was about to write this interview off as time wasted, I realized the gold mine of information I had just been privy to: tales of dirty toolboxes, smeared invoices, tuna-sandwich wrappers and empty soda cans littering her lawn, work clothes that could stand by themselves they were so covered in paint, and a briefcase that was so overstuffed it literally exploded on her kitchen counter.

In that short time period I gained an insight into the homeowner's psyche. They *do* notice, and notice big! One worker was let go due to his "foul mouth" and another because he used her expensive hand towels in the guest bathroom and left them caked with mud.

I did land the job, I did faux-finish the walls of three large rooms in her home, and, yes, it did feel like doing five-to-twenty in Sing Sing. I was instructed on every inch of paint that went on those walls and cautioned about her $9,000 Aubusson rug every day I arrived for work. She asked if my ladders were regulation (whatever that means) and insisted I leave her home if she had errands to run. As most people toss me their house keys and keypad combinations without blinking an eye, this was new to me, and a huge time waster. When I finished the job, collected my check, and was told, "All in all I'm pleased; I have a few friends who *might* be interested in your services," I drove to my favorite Japanese drive-thru and celebrated with their teriyaki supreme dinner. My husband actually brought me flowers that evening to tell me how proud he was of me for "hanging in there with Attila the Hun"!

Anyway, the moral of the story is . . . look professional, act professional, and keep your tools clean and organized; they speak volumes about you.

Meeting the Homeowner

Your first meeting with the residential client will be by phone. The first impression you make will be when the prospective client calls to ask about your services or to schedule an appointment. An upbeat professional manner on the phone and an enthusiasm for the project will set the tone for the in-person interview. While speaking to potential clients by phone, use the following guidelines:

1. Ask which area(s) of the house the client is interested in discussing. This will enable you to take along magazines, books, appropriate sample boards, and possible color selections. It saves time and is very impressive when you pull out ideas for a certain room. Children's rooms are especially great for preparing ideas ahead of time. Parents will usually tell you over the phone a theme they're considering for the child. If they don't, ask the child's age and his likes: puppies, horses, mountains, etc.

2. Schedule your appointments by phone with care, allowing yourself at least an hour to visit with the client. Allow for travel time there and back and always be on time! If you must cancel or are running late, notify the client as soon as possible. Ask the client when scheduling the appointment if she will be pressed for time or if this would be a good time for you to spend thirty minutes to an hour in her home. Avoid the dinner hour no matter how many times the client says it will be all right; that time of day is usually hectic, and many

husbands will not appreciate coming home from work to see your artwork spread across the table where dinner should be! Another time of day to watch for is when school lets out. Children hit the house like a hurricane, and the interruptions will be plentiful.

3. Try to arrange for a time when the husband will be there, too. If a financial decision has to be made, often he will need to be consulted, and this saves you time.

Note: I realize that often these roles are switched, and you'll meet with the husband and it will be the wife who'll need to be included in the financial decisions. More often than not, the person requesting the interview will make the choice on the spot and write you a check for the deposit. Most homes are two-income families these days and spouses each spend according to their whims.

4. Ask for good directions and don't be afraid to ask for clarification if you don't understand the street names. Calculate how long it will take to get there and add ten minutes for traffic delays or a missed turn. If you're going to the next town, allow plenty of time. Colorado is notorious for its road repair work due to our winters. The joke here is that Colorado has two seasons—winter and road repair. Therefore, I always leave early if I'm going to a town I haven't visited for a while, just in case there is road construction going on that I am unaware of.

Once arriving at the home, park in the street. If there is absolutely nowhere to park on the street, park in the driveway, but ask as soon as the client opens the door if it's inconvenient for your car to be there.

Shake hands with the client and thank her for inviting you to her home. As you step inside, ask if she would prefer that you remove your shoes. If she accepts, either take off your shoes or slip on a pair of surgical booties. (You have these in your briefcase for just this reason!)

If the client has pets or children, take a moment and ask their names or a little about them. People are proud of their families, and it makes a great first impression if you show you are not just there to do business. Comment on the great floor plan, the furnishings, obvious collections of Elvis Presley, antiques, wildlife art, unusual rugs, etc.

Ask if the client had a hand in the design of the home or its decoration. Make her feel special, not just a signature on a check. You will get more bookings with your personality and sincere concern for the client than with anything else. If your portfolio is professional, you've got the job over the guy who comes in and looks bored and simply asks perfunctory questions about the job.

If children do wander into the room, take a minute to talk to them. Squat down to their level and give them your full attention. If you are there to bid on their room, involve them in the decision making and compliment them on their choices. Having a child warm up to you and show you her favorite toys is always a joy—and an exchange the parent notices.

Meeting the Commercial Client

The criteria for meeting with a commercial client are slightly different from those for interviewing with a homeowner. Here are some helpful hints.

Be Professional!

Be on time! These people are busy and appreciate you considering their schedules. Dress in business attire. Show up as you would for a job interview. No tennis shoes, T-shirts, or gum.

Commercial jobs will require the most professional portfolio you have. If the cover is tired, torn, or stained, retire it! Don't waste the business owner's time: bring along only the photos and samples that benefit his type of wall space. Leave the cute stenciling and children's themes in the car unless this is the type of business that might lend itself to a children's play area.

As with the homeowner, take a moment and comment on your surroundings. Ask questions: How long has the client been in business, does he like the location, etc.

Mention any favorable comments you've heard about the client or the company. Then get down to business so as not to waste their time.

Listen

Listen! Six very important letters, for commercial clients and homeowners. *Listen* to what they'd like to see happen with the space. Underneath most observations of a room, you will hear something else: a disenchantment with the feeling the room has; or the lighting is gloomy; or the guy down the hall has such great color and atmosphere when you walk into *his* place. Don't interrupt. Save your questions for when they've finished talking. If the client is recommending a color or idea you feel is wrong for the area, whether it's a color choice that will clash with the surroundings or close in the room, or a technique you know will be cost-prohibitive, bring it up subtly, *when it's your turn.* If you have a conflicting idea, try: "I like where you're going with your ideas. You might want to consider this as a possibility because . . ." If the client is adamant, you may be stuck.

Tell him why you are recommending a different avenue—for example, "The color you're leaning toward may close in this room; how about a subtler shade of burgundy?"

Survey the Area
Walk over the site with the client and have him be specific about the area he wants painted. Take notes and make small sketches to refresh your memory and anchor down details for future reference. If it is a big area with several areas branching off from it, point to walls or columns and say, "Will this be included in the bid?"

Never assume! Clients who won't be actually painting the walls themselves tend to overlook soffits and small details that we would notice. One area often overlooked is the wall space under cabinets and desks. Pull chairs away from desks and check. Look for small areas above filing systems and coat racks. Write it all down and have them initial your layouts, noting walls, etc., that are not to be included in the price. Many times when you've painted a large area and a white piece of hallway suddenly sticks out like a sore thumb, you may hear, "I thought we were painting that, too." That's when you politely show the sketches the client initialed, and point out the red X on the hallway wall in question, designating it was not to be painted. Add, "I'd be happy to paint that for you. We're looking at $80. Is that all right?"

Working Conditions
Ask if other contractors will be on the site at the same time. Will you be working around them? Be courteous and accommodating. Simply bring up that flying dust and other's scaffolding will impede your work. You may have to stop and start as you wait for a floor to be sealed or furniture brought through.

Recently I was scrunched into a short, narrow hallway with three other workers. As I tried to paint a fox running through a line of aspen trees, I had an electrician straddling a ladder over my head, while another one worked on the outlets behind my back. The gentleman staining the trim work was a mere two feet away. I like working around construction because I enjoy interacting and laughing with "the guys." However, your efficiency will be greatly impeded if all of you end up in the same area at the same time. Find out ahead of time the scheduling of *all* the work crews for the project and try and work out a time line that will benefit everyone. There will be more on dealing with contractors in chapter 6.

One of my favorite commercial projects included a series of pediatric dental clinics across the United States. I loved working with the staff and patients. While painting the Hygiene and Ortho bays, hallways and waiting areas, however, there were many obstacles to overcome. In one clinic, the entire west wall was covered in waist-high cabinets, which meant I had to lean over them to paint the walls behind them, or even stand on them for higher areas. This is back-breaking work after awhile and really slows you down. I was working around dental operations and being careful not to bump clients who were in a prone position in the dental chairs only inches from my chair. The hallways were a constant crunch of staff and patients and families, many stopping to talk to me or ask for a business card. I dearly love interacting with people and laughing with them. Just remember to take everything into account when you are bidding a commercial site. Allow for interruptions. Ask which areas you will not be welcome in during operating hours (no pun intended).

Also find out ahead of time if the outlets will be "hot." This is the term electricians use to indicate whether an outlet has power or not. If not, there goes your radio, cell phone charger, electric pencil sharpener, etc. Find out if there will be any running water available. I've had to carry in my own water in 5-gallon buckets on more than one occasion. Will there be lighting? If not, you may have shorter hours when the sunlight's not available, or charge extra for a generator and lights.

Determine the company's operating hours if it is a business already open. You may have to work evenings and weekends if they can't have you painting around customers. Try to accommodate their constraints without becoming inconvenienced yourself. Some artists charge more if they're required to give up family time and their only days off. This is fair to ask for compensation in order to accommodate unusual working hours.

Sketch Fees

If the contract is for a mural, you may need to charge extra if the clients want to see a sketch before awarding you the job and deposit. I charge $30 an hour for sketches. This fee can be deducted from the deposit if you get the job. There will be artists hungry enough for work that they will do the drawings for free in hopes of landing the job. You'll have to decide how badly you want the bid.

Bids and Schedules

Type up your bid on your professional letterhead and keep a copy for yourself.

Itemize all parts of the job with their individual prices so there are no misunderstandings. (A sample of an itemized bid is included in chapter 10.) If you have to travel out of town, list travel expenses separately. Remember: you are charging for gas and time; the hours you spend on the road could be used generating income painting a wall somewhere. If you are expected to add a protective sealant to walls or floors, add that cost separately, plus the added time to apply them. Floor sealants usually require two to three coats at twenty-four-hour intervals.

Let the client know where you are currently in scheduling. For example: "I just want you to know that I am booked until May 11th. Will that work for you?"

Find out now, while you're interviewing for the job, if the owner has to be open for business at a required time or if he has a deadline to meet. Your next opening may be outside those parameters, and you would be wasting his time and yours. I've found that once a client has seen my work and we have established a good rapport, he is usually willing to wait, unless it is entirely out of his hands. Therefore, go into a commercial bid with your best foot forward. Clients may ask for references. I usually include, along with the itemized bid, a short sheet with the name of other businesses I have painted. It all cements that valuable impression of professionalism.

You're On!

You've introduced yourself to the client, chatted with the kids, petted the dog, and mentioned the Picasso hanging above the fireplace. Your clothes are impeccable, your samples ready to go.

I would like to add a word here about body language: keep your hands and posture relaxed and open. If your arms are tightly folded or your hands jammed into your pockets, it gives the impression that you are nervous or uncomfortable. Shake hands immediately upon arriving and keep your hands expressive as you point out walls or photos. Eye contact is extremely important and implies confidence and interest in the client; people have a hard time connecting with someone who is constantly studying the floor or her shoes.

Ask if the client would like to sit down and look at your portfolio first or take a look at the room she wants finished. Let her take the lead. It's a pretty even split here: some will show you the room and point out problems with it or suggest a theme they're interested in pursuing. Others will say, "Why don't we sit down at the kitchen table and you can show me your work." If they ask you to decide which you'd rather do first, I usually choose to look at the room first. There's a reason for this: if I see the area ahead of time, I can later emphasize those photos in my portfolio that hit on the things they mentioned in the room. If bidding a mural and the client would like to price one surrounding the entire room but is a little nervous about cost, I tell her I can bid it two ways: (1) with a mural wrapping the room and ceiling, and (2) pulling in elements around the room but not necessarily covering every square inch. Then, when we sit down to look over my work, I show her pictures of both examples along with a sample price for each technique. You'll get a lot of information ahead of time by seeing the room and *listening* to the client's fears and wants. Then you can alleviate her fears with pictures that speak to her concerns, and establish the exact design for the room.

Once seated at the table, open your portfolio and go over your work. Skip over photos that don't really address her needs unless they amply show off your eye for detail and design. Don't go too fast. Allow her to ask questions and look over the work. Emphasize the pictures that nail the ideas you discussed while looking over the room. Point out that these are all custom-done projects and the client doesn't have to choose something from these pages; they are simply to represent your work. Brainstorm a little. Several times I've been asked if a color or layout could be changed, when clients were looking at my photos. It was then I realized they thought the pictures before them were their only choices in what I could paint. Ask them if they have any questions as you go along. Don't assume they know what the different treatments of faux finishing are or how a mural is rendered.

Many clients need to be led and are hoping you'll tell them what they'll fall in love with! This takes some tact. Feel them out to see just how much they want your ideas or simply an embellishment of their own. Indecisive clients want help. They won't come right out and say, "I'm an idiot . . . I don't know Crazy Horse Red from Lemon Meringue Yellow" (although some have made similar self-deprecating statements). You'll sense if they want you to take the lead. Assure them that 90 percent of your clients don't have a clue, either, about all the wonderful finishes and mural options out there. This usually relieves their mind and they feel freer to address their fears.

Well, you've got their attention, you know the room they want painted and a little of their hopes and dreams for that room . . . now what?

What Do I Do First?

First, take in all your surroundings. What colors do they tend to lean toward?

Are burgundy and hunter green popping up throughout the house? What style of furnishings do they have? Colonial, European, country, contemporary, a mixture? What's on the walls? Paintings, their kid's artwork, silk floral swags, a collage of family pictures? What color is the carpet? This is more important than you may think and is often overlooked. You are dealing with four planes when you paint, not just the walls you're contracted for. They all work to form one cohesive whole. If the carpet color is taupe, then the wall color you choose will have to work with that color, not fight it. You'll know the minute you lay your sample board on the carpet whether they will work harmoniously together.

Where is the light coming from in the room? Do the windows face east, west, north, south, or a combination? Determining the light is your first task when deciding upon a faux finish. It will greatly affect your color choice! North- and east-facing windows typically receive the weakest and coldest light. The sun rises in the east, then steadily makes its way toward the west, reaching midway around noon. This means the light coming in your north and east windows is feeble morning light that won't be there long. This weak light can make a room painted in blues and grays cold and unwelcoming. These rooms need warm colors to offset the light. Windows facing south and west get the strong noon and afternoon light and can handle cool tones of blues, gray-greens and taupes. The *amount* of light is also important. If the window is small or obstructed by outdoor trees or heavy curtains, this will also affect the *mood* in the room and the color selection. Does the site have lamp or overhead lighting; halogen or track? Take a close look at the room. It may need light, bright colors to reflect more light back. It may need a higher-sheen paint as well.

> **TIP:** Wherever fluorescent lighting is used, take special care to check the sample board under it. It can change a subtle wheat color to a garish yellow-orange!

Are there any problem areas? Repair work needed? Ceiling corners that can't be reached because of a jutting or built-in mantel? Are the stairs workable for ladders? Are there heavy pieces of furniture that the homeowner has no way of moving? Can the refrigerator be pulled out easily to paint that three-inch space you can barely see above it? Has that huge gold, ornate mirror over the sofa been molly-bolted to the wall? Will that hanging ledge support your weight if you have to crawl out onto it?

What wall texture will you be working with? We discussed this already. Feel the wall; if it's dry or chalky, it is probably flat paint, and you will need to charge more for the extra time needed to get a silky finish, or choose a faux finish that requires a solid base coat as its first step and paint it in a satin sheen. Is it a knockdown, orange peel, or flat wall? You will spend more time painting a mural on a flat wall than one with some texture. This is because a flat wall shows every brush stroke and requires more coats of paint to get a solid look. Flat walls are great for showing off patterned fauxs, such as ragging, cheesecloth, or chamois, and for gorgeous Venetian plasters, marbles, and metallics. For a beautiful Old World finish, it's hard to beat a dramatic troweled plaster or knockdown texture. The wall's surface will dictate which samples you proffer.

Ask where they would like you to do your cleanup and get water for mixes. Some homeowners frown on paint in their kitchen sink and will usually direct you to a laundry room if they have one. Take your own paper towels, lots of them, and leave the area spotless. I usually take along a cleanser and clean the sink after. This is also critical in a commercial establishment. Always ask where they would like you to clean up. Don't just help yourself to the public bathroom or break room—always ask.

Choosing Colors

All right, now for the hard part! How do you pick a color to suggest for their wall(s)? A study in color theory and some practice with a color wheel would be immensely helpful. Here're a few tricks to help you get started!

1. Look at the room you're in. If the couch or window coverings are fabric, take a color from that. First, ask if these furnishings and coverings are going to stay. Look at the fabric and select the softest background color, such as butterscotch, beige, taupe, etc. If the client wants to go bold, choose one of the primary colors splashed across the fabric, like that big bold navy-blue carnation in the center of the draperies. Again, the lighting in the room will determine what color to use. If a soft sage-green color would pull out the fabric colors and work well with the other colors in the room, including the carpet and wood trim, try that on a sample

board for them to consider. I usually offer to do several boards in different techniques and color intensity so the client can see the difference between subtle and *ka-boom!* Better yet, have several colored sample boards with you to hold up and help the process of elimination along. Some people detest blues and yellows. Save yourself some time and ask if there are certain colors to be avoided.

2. If there are no fabrics to choose from, look at carpet color. A taupe carpet goes well with colors that have a gray tint to them. The gray-blues and greens work well, as does a burgundy with a gray undertone. Pure colors are usually too intense and offer too much contrast. Obviously, a neutral carpet in beiges, tans, or off-whites will go well with anything. If it's a hardwood floor, be careful. The wood color will dictate what paint to use. Some woods have an orange cast; mahoganies have a reddish cast, etc. Lay your sample board on the floor and see what happens to your color. It should be obvious if it's wrong.

3. You can pull a color from a plate collection in the dining room, border paper in the kitchen, the matting on large paintings in the living room, a bedspread, masonry around the fireplace, etc. There is my "go-to" paint if all else fails. It is a soft wheat color that's not too yellow and not too tan. It goes with everything! Sherwin Williams has this in its color selection and it's called, of all things, Whole Wheat. It brings out the color of everything it comes into contact with, and a green plant placed against it is a rare thing of beauty. It has enough golden tones to warm a weak-lighted room and adds lush color to a well-lit one.

4. Don't hesitate to ask to take a pillow or fabric sample home with you to match a color for a sample board. Encase it in plastic during your painting time. Tile samples or wood trim are also useful.

Here's the part where you're going to love me! There is a rule of thumb about fabric and room color selection: Look at a piece of fabric with several colors; a floral-patterned one is good. Usually the color found in the largest amount in the fabric should go on the largest area of the room; namely, the walls or the floor.

The second largest amount would go to the second largest area, such as large pieces of furniture or drapes. The smaller color sections would be used for lampshades, throw pillows, and accent pieces. If you have a piece of fabric whose main color, when you squint at it, is forest green, and the room is too small, too dark, or the owner doesn't want that dramatic a color on their walls, try a tinted-down version in a soft mossy green, or go to a neutral, like a warm beige or taupe.

You can look to the color's complementary color on the color wheel for help. Green's complementary hue is red or orange. Would a soft peach color go in the room to play background for the fabric? Odds are there is a red or orange offspring in the fabric, if green is the main color.

There is no substitute for learning all you can about color and its theories. Hundreds of books are out there under interior decorating in your bookstores. Some are dedicated solely to understanding color. Study magazines geared to interior decorating, and study why they paired a certain color with a certain room's elements. This becomes a fun game but can be addictive. I study restaurant surroundings to see what they've done with the walls, fabric, etc. A little experience and you'll be picking colors out of midair. Let the client look through your paint sample fan you acquired at the paint store. Hold different colors up to the drapes, furnishings, etc. Narrow down their preferences to three choices and begin with those. Offer to do sample boards in those three colors and decide upon a technique: ragging, sponge, etc. Set a date to return with the boards and see how they work. Always have the client leave them up overnight to see the effect changing light has on them.

Special Considerations for Murals

If you're bidding a mural, take a good look at the wall surface to see if there are major nail holes, cracks, etc., that need repair before you start. Ask if the furniture in the room is where it will stay, as this will affect your mural's placement. You don't want to render a gorgeous underwater ocean scene and have them place a crib in front of it, blocking the best fish you ever painted in your life. Notice the lighting, both artificial and natural. A dark-blue ocean may be too gloomy for a small, dimly lit room. If they are adamant about the scene they want, try pressing them to add better light fixtures; track lighting is inexpensive and showcases your work.

Figure the placement of all furniture, window seats, accessories, etc. to determine the best layout of your mural's elements. Don't forget soffits, light fans, and recesses when "taking it all in."

Use your particular method of bidding: by the square foot, flat fee, or by the hour. This is covered in the next section. If you are going by square footage, this is where you whip out the tape measure. Don't use cloth tapes; use metal or those wonderful folding wooden ones, or better yet, laser tools.

Go over colors, both those they want included and those they don't. Take a look around the room and notice bedspreads, curtains, painted furniture, etc. You don't want your mural clashing with the other colors going on. It always helps to tie a theme together with what's happening in the fabrics. If the bedspread is baseball ornamented and they want a beach scene, that's fine, but a room looks more pulled together if a consistent theme exists. If the mural is in a living room, laundry room, or breakfast nook, again, play off existing materials and motifs. There is a jarring effect when too many themes are brought into play.

If the client has an idea of the scene a mural is to depict, ask whether she has any pictures picked out or do you need to do some research. If you've brought books, pull these out and see if you can get the client narrowed down to a few ideas. You can't bid the room until you know what you're painting. If you sense you'll be putting in a lot of time researching ideas, add this charge in your bid. Explain to them beforehand that if you do all the legwork, it bites into your time, and you'll have to charge accordingly. Encourage clients to do as much of the "looking" as possible, since they will know what they're looking for better than you will. All of chapter 9 is dedicated to murals.

These tips on what to do first pertain to residential and commercial clients. The rules of color selection and what to look for apply to both.

Evaluate the Job Site

Take a good, hard look at the overall job. Is the budget worthwhile for the amount of time and travel involved? What about the nature of the project? Are the ceilings eighteen feet high? Are there obstacles to work around that will be a strain on your back or neck? Lugging in huge ladders and arranging for and moving scaffolding are huge headaches and time wasters. Will the client be on the premises and watching you the whole time? Will children and pets be running around? Will you be working around new construction—painters, plumbers, floor people, cabinet installers, etc.? These will all slow you down. Try to schedule your work around these people so that you are not in the same room at the same time.

How about the conditions outside the project site? New construction usually means dirt parking lots or driveways. If it rains or snows, are you in for one muddy trek in and out? Will you have to park a block away and haul all your equipment a good distance? Is the neighborhood safe; would you be nervous walking to your car after dark? If you see a portable outdoor toilet on the site, odds are good you'll be using it . . . along with Red, the burly tile guy. Bring your own toilet paper and sanitary wipes!

Some new construction demands you wear a hard hat at all times. This is fun when you're trying to see out from under the bill that keeps sliding down into your eyes. You can argue all you want with the foreman, but OSHA dictates the rules and he'll kick you off the property if you don't comply. Goggles are sometimes enforced as well.

Will there be a heater if the electricity hasn't been turned on yet? Even if your fingers haven't turned brittle, your paints will, if exposed to cold temperatures for very long. There is no reason why you should be expected to perform your specialized skill under inadequate conditions. Insist on heat, light, and clean surroundings.

I was painting a large mural a few years ago for a new barbecue restaurant that was behind schedule in the construction phase of things. As a result, I was painting the wall while buzz saws whirred around me and heating ducts were installed directly overhead. At one point, a large chunk of sheet metal came whizzing past my ear and landed in my paint tray. Mr. Buzz Saw had slipped on his workbench. (Please reread the disability and liability insurance section in chapter 2!) If you work around any kind of new construction, you can write a few good stories of your own!

If children and pets are to be a part of the package, ask that the pets be kept in another room or outside while you paint; not because you're mean, but for the pet's protection as well. I have had both cats and dogs step into my paint tray or swipe a tail across a freshly painted wall. A large gray tabby crawled beneath my tarp and I narrowly missed stepping on its back. When you're on ladders, children and pets can be a work risk. Explain this politely to the owner. One that usually settles it for moms is when I mention the paints will not come out of their children's clothes. Will you be expected to work around naptime if you're painting in the child's room or the near vicinity?

You can't ask too many questions about your working conditions. Write down any particular demand of the client on the invoice and have her initial it.

Evaluate the Client

You will be dealing with a lot of different personalities out there in the world of painting. I am pleased to report that 92 percent of them will be a treat to work around. The other 8 percent will cause an early onset of the graying process and an increase in the consumption of antacids. They will be the clients that build your character and test your mettle. They will call you an average of three times a day for the three weeks preceding their project's due date to ask some of the most amazing questions you'll ever hear. Here's a little of the flavor: "Will I need to fold my clothes if you're going to use the laundry room sink for wash-up?" "My husband refuses to leave the living room during the time you'll be here because the Broncos are playing the Raiders for the playoffs. You'll just have to work around him!" And, my personal favorite, "If we paint the kitchen and dinette in a peach color, will my plastic avocadoes clash with it?"

If you have a bad feeling about a client, let the job go! Trust your instincts. A check is not worth the stress and aggravation. If you meet with someone who begins barking out orders like a Gestapo official or has a mile-long list of requirements that must be met, I'd walk. If you're meeting with a woman who can talk for ten minutes without drawing breath, think it over carefully. The nonstop talkers are big time-eaters and will usually stay right by your elbow the entire time telling you about their niece's liver transplant and Aunt Gloria's ingrown toenail problem. (You think I'm kidding? I wish I were!!) The first-impression rule works both ways, so get a good feel of whom you'll be working around.

The flip side is those wonderful human beings who remind you of why you chose this business to start with. They have a radio waiting for you, a bowl of pretzels and a soda set out on the kitchen counter, and the furniture and wall hangings all moved out of the way. I have been tossed keys to golf carts, flown across country, and put up in condos that would dazzle your eyes out. Cards, gifts, phone messages, and flowers that have made me cry are all part of this terrific career. You give your clients 100 percent, and they'll bowl you over with their gratitude. Good customer service is getting harder to come by . . . *incredible* customer service is nonexistent . . . until *you* come along!!

When to Show the Samples

We've already covered your samples and correct way to show them. A brief word here about timing. Once you've shown your portfolio, assessed the room(s) to be painted, and listened to the client's needs, bring out the samples at that time, not before. You can overwhelm a client if you don't do things in order. You may be tempted to run and grab the sample board with the denim-blue color wash right in the middle of her complaining that the dark blue in the room is confining, but wait until she's through. It looks pushy and rude to interrupt and race off to hurry things along. Here's the order of things:

1. Introduce yourself and make small talk.
2. Ask to see the room(s) you're bidding on.
3. Assess the room and its lighting.
4. Show your portfolio.
5. Make color recommendations based on room's elements.
6. Show samples that will illustrate your color selections.
7. Go back around the room and carefully estimate the job.
8. Bid the job with an itemized invoice.
9. Schedule a date on your calendar.
10. Ask for a half-down deposit to reserve the date.

Chapter 5 will cover numbers 7–10. For the purposes of this section, notice where your sample board presentation falls.

Check Out the Walls

In your hurry to bid a job you might take a cursory look at the walls, determine their texture and their sheen, and feel you're done. Au contraire! Take the time now to peek behind pictures, drapes, and furniture to evaluate the condition of the walls. The client needs to be notified now if repair work needs to be done. Faux finishes are delicate glazes, and patched spackle work, large nail holes, and wallpaper adhesive residue will all affect their final appearance.

Unprimed spackle and adhesive residue will show up in ugly patches through your glaze. Large cracks from the house settling will also show through. Ask your client if she wants to pay you to do the repair work or will she take care of it. It should be done at least a day in advance, to allow cure time for the spackle and paint. If spackle is used, once it's dry, it should be sanded, primed, and base-coated to match the walls.

> **TIP:** Make sure any painted surfaces of the wall are in one consistent color. If you're doing a one-step glaze, discolorations from different colored touch-up paints will show through.

If the client balks at this prep work or cost, explain you can't guarantee a professional look without these needed repairs, and she'll be wasting her money.

One final note on checking out walls: peek at the ceiling line around the room. Some are not plumb, and you may spend some time up there with a liner brush filling in gaps your paint shield could not compensate for.

The Client's Responsibilities

1. Move all furniture, wall hangings, draperies, etc., out of your way.
2. Repair all cracks, remove wallpaper adhesive residue, etc., if agreed upon.
3. Make arrangements for pets and children to be out of the way.
4. Arrange for a cleanup sink to be free of obstacles, such as clothes, dishes, toys, etc.
5. Provide a key, keypad combination, or open door if she will not be at home.

6. Provide a phone number where she can be reached during the day in case of questions or an emergency.
7. Let you know if others will be dropping by or packages arriving while you are on the premises.
8. Supply floor plans if needed.
9. Approve samples, bids, and schedules, and sign off on them.
10. Pay the agreed-upon monies on time. An interest charge should be stipulated in the bid if the client fails to pay on the agreed-upon date. List when interest will begin accruing.
11. Renegotiate any added materials, painting, or changes from the original bid. Watch out for the "Oh, as long as you're here, could you just add . . ." or "This would only take you a minute, so could you add . . ."
12. Ensure comfort level while painter is on site. Adequate heat, lighting, and dust-free conditions should prevail.

Points to be Negotiated with the Client

1. If the work is canceled, stipulate if the deposit is refundable in whole or part, and the deadline for cancellation, beyond which the deposit becomes nonrefundable. Do they owe you money for samples, meetings, etc.?
2. If you are working on furniture or any other offsite projects, do you want to charge the client for transportation of the piece to and from the property?
3. Ask whether or not supplies can be stored on site overnight, out of the way, or if you'll have to pack them up at the end of the day.
4. Ask whether paint odors are a problem, if it is alright to open windows, etc. Is anyone in the home asthmatic or dealing with other health issues that sanding or paint fumes might exacerbate?
5. Ask clients how they want their doors locked if you leave and they are not there. Are you expected to let animals back into the room, accept packages delivered while you're on site, etc.?
6. Explain to the clients how long the job will take to dry, and when it is appropriate to let children and pets back into the room.

Some artists print these conditions up and hand them to their clientele at the close of a successful interview. It doesn't hurt for *both* parties to know what's expected of them!

5

HOW TO BID A JOB

When it comes to bidding a project, most artists panic. I have calls from seasoned veterans asking me how to bid jobs. They tell me they are always underbidding jobs out of panic that they won't win the bid, or estimating too high and losing the project to someone else. Estimating projects is a tricky task. Time and experience are the main tools needed to perfect this part of the business, and even then you may lose some.

Feeling out the competition is your main advantage to getting a good hold of the bidding-war situation. With murals, you'll find the competition drops considerably, unless you live in a huge metropolis and have several Yellow Pages full of muralists. Usually, you're in a select group, and then your work will sell the job or it won't. When it comes to creative endeavors, such as hand-painted walls and furniture, the bid is secondary to your ability to create masterpieces.

You can have a friend call around to different faux painters or muralists and try to get a rough idea of what they charge. Most will tell you they have to come out to the site to get a feel for the walls, area, and working conditions . . . I do. I don't give bids, even rough ones, over the phone. Too many factors that determine the bid's outcome are involved. Besides, "eyeballing" the area is my preference for estimating a job.

You might try to get a feel for the estimating field by asking interior designers what the going rate for faux finishing is, but again, they may say each artist is different and there is no blanket scale to work from. Bidding for murals will be covered in chapter 9.

With that said, here are three methods for estimating jobs to help you along:

Three Methods for Estimating: Flat Fee, Square Footage, or By the Hour

There are three methods used in estimating fees for faux and mural work:

1. **The flat-fee estimate:** A total price is given for the completion of a job with the cost of materials included. This is what I call "eyeball-ing" the job. The materials are included, although you'll itemize them on your invoice to figure your tax on supplies.
2. **The square-foot quote:** A specific charge per square foot of wall based on the technique chosen. Materials are usually included.
3. **By the hour:** You are paid a set fee based on actual hours worked. Usually this is for a specific part of a job where you are hired on a temporary basis. Materials are billed separately.

My personal preference is the flat-fee bid. I go in and look at the area to be painted, taking into consideration the size of the wall, texture, technique or difficulty of the mural or faux, and whether it will require special equipment or extra time for high ceilings, etc. I try to make anywhere from $380 to $600 a day (there will be times when you'll make as much as $1,000 in one day, but I use an average, when bidding, roughly $400 per day). I determine how many days I think the job will take and times that by my daily-wage criteria. This is not hard. After only one job, you should have a pretty good idea of how long a room will take you to paint using *that* technique on *that* kind of wall. If you are asked to do a more complicated technique, add more time.

With a mural, it is a little harder to guesstimate how long it will take you to render it. Painting landscapes will go faster than painting wildlife, and painting wildlife will go faster than painting people. No two murals are ever the same, due to the amount of detail involved. You may want to spend more time making a lake look real, or shading Winnie the Pooh to look like he just jumped out of a Disney film. Do the best you can figuring out if this will take you a day, two days, two and a half days, etc. Then use your daily wage criteria:

$400 a day × 3 days = $1,200 for the job. Remember, your materials are included in this price unless you prefer to bid them separately. You will still need to write them down on the invoice in order to figure tax for Uncle Sam.

Add a little extra time in the beginning of your career as a safety margin until you get the hang of estimating the amount of time involved in a project. Allow for prep and cleanup time. Cleanup usually takes 20–30 minutes, whereas prep time (taping off, setting up tarps, plastic drops, talking to the client, mixing paint, etc.) can take 30–45 minutes or more.

The square-foot bid is hard because texture comes into play, as well as factoring in doors, windows, fireplaces, etc. It is too binding for me; and to measure a mural by the square foot is ludicrous.

Estimating Time

If trying to "eyeball" a room and determine a price seems too hard at first, try breaking it down to one wall at a time. How long would you guess it would take you to paint wall A? An hour? Two hours? Jot down a note that shows wall A/2 hrs. Next, wall B. How long? Well, there's a fireplace sitting in the middle of it, so not as long as wall A. It would probably take . . . say, 1 ½ hours. Note: wall B/1 ½ hrs. (FYI: It *can* sometimes take longer to paint around fireplaces, windows, and doors than it does to paint an uninterrupted wall. Don't let the client try and tell you that due to all the built-ins, you shouldn't need to charge as much for that wall. If you are taping those intrusions off or cutting in around them, they eat up time.) Wall C is full of windows, so maybe an hour to glaze that one: wall C/1 hr. Wall D is a half wall above the entrance to the kitchen but we'll say an hour to give ourselves some breathing room: wall D/1 hr. Now, add them up. A is 2 hrs. + B is 1 ½ hrs. + C is 1 hr. + D is 1 hr. = 5 ½ hrs. For me, 5 ½ hours is a typical workday. I usually work between five and seven hours, with six as an average. The work you're doing is physically and mentally straining. Anything over 6–7 hours, and your creativity will suffer. (So will your back!) So, 5 ½ to 6 hours would be a $380–$400 day (your daily wage criteria), and you could bid the room accordingly. See, not so hard. Now, let's break it down even further:

If it is a three-step faux process with a base coat and two more glazes applied, how long will the base coat take to apply? Use the method above to break down each wall.

> **TIP:** It takes much longer to paint a wall in a solid paint color than it does to glaze a wall. Solid paint takes more prep time in taping off, it usually requires two coats (or more if it's a strong pigment like red or green), and the drying time is longer. Bid plenty of time for a base coat, about double for the time it would take you to simply glaze it.

Now you have the time for the base coat, figure the time needed for the first glaze, breaking down each wall as we did above. Now add the time for the second glaze. In many glazing techniques, the subsequent glazes take up less and less wall, with the previous glazes left untouched. Some require you to glaze over the entire area you just finished in the previous step. If you're covering every square inch in all three steps, you will literally be covering that wall three times. Bid accordingly. Allow extra time for interruptions, errors, or a slow drying time where you'll have to make small talk with the client until the wall is dry enough to move on to the next step.

If you feel safer doing it by the square foot, the going rate is $2 per square foot and higher. You can call around and try to get quotes from other faux finishers to test the bidding waters. A typical rule of thumb is to bid 25 percent higher than a regular interior painter would charge for a room. Call some area painters, give them a room dimension, such as 10' × 17', and ask what they would ballpark that area. You will probably hear that they'll have to come and see the room to determine the wall's texture, etc., but give it a try. Your paint-store dealer may have an idea what the going rate is in the area for painter's hours.

You will need to charge extra if the wall needs to be primed before applying a base coat. A primer coat is required if the existing color contrasts strongly with the new color or if the existing surface has an oil-based finish or is contaminated. A contaminated surface is one that been exposed to long-term nicotine, ink, or smoke from fireplaces or a house fire. You will also need primer if it is new drywall or bare wood, or if you are asked to paint over brick as found in a fireplace surround project. Don't forget to figure in prep time and cleanup time, travel, etc. Add 10 to15 percent more time to allow for delays.

> TIP: Allow extra time if you're working around furniture that was merely pulled away from the wall instead of removed from the room. If you can tell the parking arrangements will be inconvenient, factor that in. Painting ceilings, moldings, curved or carved surfaces, awkward access to surfaces to be treated, working with an inexperienced client or decorator, and walls eighteen feet or higher, are all time busters. Look over the area carefully and factor in all these things. Don't forget pets and children wandering through the site or a talkative client.

I use the term *decorative painting* for projects other than faux and murals. Stenciling, hand-painted furniture, room screens, painted lampshades, wooden cornices, floor-cloths, hand-painted floors or tiles, etc., fall in the category of decorative painting. Knowing how to bid these jobs will come with experience. The flat-fee or "eyeballing" method will be the rule of thumb with the exception of stenciling. Some stencil artists bid these by the square foot or linear foot, as they usually run along soffits or adorn walls in specific areas. Don't forget to multiply your stencils by the number of overlays.

Decorative painters usually run into more supply costs, as they are factoring in wood for the room screens; polyurethane sealer for the floors; sanding, sealing, and priming materials for furniture; and canvas for floor-cloths. Many stencils are 2–8 overlays and require moving over the same area the number of overlays involved. Take your time and write down all the materials involved in the project (don't forget tape, pencils, adhesive, sandpaper, etc.). Then, *carefully*, decide how many hours you think the project will take you.

> TIP: Room screens and furniture will require drying time for primers and sealers. These usually need to be sanded between coats and tack-clothed. Figure in this time not only for the bid but for the delivery date you promise the client. Floors require two or three urethane coats at twenty-four-hour time intervals. Look over each step of the process needed for the project and factor that in. If you're painting furniture, room screens, or other large items, do you have the necessary vehicle to haul these back and forth to the client? Have you added time for pickup and delivery, or are you "throwing that in"?

In chapter 10, we will cover the new painting techniques for walls, floors, ceilings, furnishings, and more, complete with set-up and time needs so you can bid them accordingly.

What to Look For

Here's a quick checklist of what you're looking for in order to give a correct estimate:

- What texture are the walls? Will their texture slow things down or speed them up?
- Do the walls need repair? If so, are you in charge of repairs? Include this in the bid. Don't forget your cost in spackle, sandpaper, etc.
- How high are the walls? Climbing up and down an extension ladder takes a lot longer and eats time.
- Are there any obstructions, such as overhangs, oversized mantels, ledges, elaborate window coverings that must be removed or worked around? Are there built-ins, such as bookcases, entertainment centers, etc., that will be difficult to work around? If you're in a kitchen, does the island counter allow room for a ladder's width? Will you have to stand on counters to reach areas a ladder can't? Are there strange window configurations making ladder access difficult?
- What sheen is the wall painted in now? Eggshell, flat, semi-gloss, gloss? If you're doing a one-step glaze over a flat wall, the dull base will hinder you. In chapter 6 I have a tip to help with this problem.
- What are the floor conditions? If the floors are hardwood, and you'll be up on an extension ladder, you'll need a nonskid mat under your ladder's feet. If it's carpeting, extra tarps are always a good idea: ones with plastic or rubber leak-proof bottoms.
- Will you be working around blinds that the owner does not want removed due to the special installation required to put them up?
- How much taping off is required?
- Will furniture be removed completely from the room or are you working around obstacles?
- What about time constraints? Do the owners only want you in their home or business during certain hours, thereby cutting into your day? Does the commercial client need you to work after operating

hours? Will you be required to leave if the client has errands or is expecting company? Always ask!

- Is there a source of running water, or will you have to cart in your own? This will slow you down as you try to clean out sponges and brushes in cold, dirty water as well as carrying it in your vehicle without spilling it everywhere.
- Will there be adequate light, or will you incur the expense of a generator and lights? Factor this into the bid.
- Will there be heat if cold is a factor? Again, add the cost of a heater and possibly a generator.
- Are the outlets "hot," or will you need to find a different source of electricity?
- Will you be working around other laborers? They can slow you down, and you are often sharing outlets, cleanup sources, the client's feedback time, etc.
- Add in children, pets, talkative clients, and neighbors, and your own cell phone interruptions when figuring time.
- This is a good time to note any damage already done to the area you'll be working in, so you can't be blamed for it later. Note any stains on the carpet, wall repairs needed, scraped floors, etc. Bring them to the client's attention and include them in the contract.
- Don't forget travel, prep time, and cleanup when figuring costs.

Bidding Long Distance Jobs

As your business grows you will probably be asked to leave the comfort of your home for another destination. This may be the next city, the next state, or the next country! These jobs require you to sharpen your pencil when it comes to charging for your time and expenses. Some residential jobs in another city or state may offer to put you up in the home or condo you will be painting. This can be very nice and I have really enjoyed this type of set-up. The clients save money by not paying for a hotel room for you or for a car rental. I prefer it because all my equipment can remain on-site instead of lugging things from a hotel room and in and out of a car. The hospitality has been wonderful and usually includes meals, joining the family for TV in the evenings, and removes the lonely feeling you can sometimes get from being in a hotel in a strange city.

In those situations, you would charge for air fare, or car travel expense such as gas, mileage maintenance or car rental charges. Keep track of your mileage and decide on a fair rate for maintenance, oil, gas, etc. Ask an accountant what would be a fair rate. If driving, you can charge for food while on the road.

If you are flying in, then you would charge for air fare to and from the site, shuttle charges if incurred, car rental if needed, food for three meals a day during the duration of the project, hotel costs if you are not staying on site, and even specialty clothing if needed or special equipment. The client pays for all materials. Since my special brushes kit travels with me everywhere, I do not charge for brushes unless specialty ones are required. The client pays for any equipment rentals such as scaffolding, ladders, heaters, extra lighting, etc.

Go over all of these details when negotiating the contract. Do not let anyone get away with saying, "Well, we can discuss all this when you get there." This is a very tricky area and all avenues need to be spelled out, including extra charges for unforeseen delays, misinformation concerning the condition of the site, walls, climate, etc. Often you will not see the site you are flying to ahead of time and you must put a contingency clause in the contract that your bid is for the job described and have the client be very specific about the working conditions, age of the home or business, condition of the walls, other construction that may be going on, heat, lighting, water sources, operating hours, etc. Get it all in writing. If possible obtain a floor plan of the building. Have the client stipulate in the plan which areas are to be painted and put a red X on the walls that are not included in the bid. Find out about pets, visitors, smokers, and anything else you can think of that might impact your work.

Finally, you will be charging for your time while traveling. This is time you could have been working on other projects, so make sure they understand you are billing traveling time and any other time that takes you away from a typical working day. Be fastidious about keeping receipts for your gas, food, car rental, car rental insurance, hotels, buses, supplies, etc.

Landing the Job!

Once you've evaluated the job site and established a great rapport with the clients, go over their choices once again, if they've already indicated color and theme preference as we discussed in chapter 4. Are they excited at this point, or showing some hesitancy? Don't ignore their little doubts and fears. These are real and may surface again once you've started painting. Address the doubts *now* and give them proper consideration. Perhaps they are still not sure how the color will impact the room or if it is right for them. Maybe the stenciling or mural is a new stretch for them, and they're worried it will be "too much" for the room. Go over everything until they look relaxed and confident; never bulldoze them just to get the bid. Some clients will require a couple of trips back with samples, pictures, or sketches. Charge accordingly for these extra considerations. One idea that has worked well for me is to offer to show them the same wall color and technique I've rendered in another client's home. Most clients, especially if they were pleased with you and your work, are open to having someone come take a peek if scheduled ahead of time. Having the reticent client see how the paint technique works in a real setting with furnishings, fabrics, lighting, etc., is a huge bonus. In the past three weeks, I've had four clients over to my own home to show them different techniques and colors I've painted on my walls. I sold all four after showing them "up close and personal" how a room benefits from color and murals.

> **TIP:** If you are a homeowner, paint your home and use it as your showcase. Try to incorporate different techniques to illustrate the benefits of ragging, plaster, chamois, etc.

Now that you've gone over everything, and the clients feel confident about the proposed project, sit down with them and go over the itemized bid. I usually walk the rooms I'm bidding on one more time before I sit down with them to double check my projections and take one more peek at the walls. Take the blank invoice with you and list each room with a short description of what you'll be doing in it, color names, glazing technique, etc., and list the price projection. Do this for each area you're bidding, for example:

1. Kitchen: Venture Green/2-tone sponge-on/All walls w/soffit $320[1]
2. Dinette: Amish Linen/Color wash/sponge-on/All walls $280
3. Guest Bath: Bronze/4-tone w/gold, terra-cotta, umber wash $400

---

[1] If you're using the square-foot bidding method, put the wall's measurements here. The total will reflect your area measurement times your $2-per-square-foot price. Ex: Wall A: 8' × 14' = 110 sq. ft. × $2 = $220.

List any walls you are not required to paint, and have the client initial it. If this requires a sketch on a separate sheet of paper attached to the invoice, then by all means do it. You will come across as deceptive later if the client wants to know why you didn't include the wall to the left of the doorway and you tell her it wasn't in the bid. A sketch with a red X on that wall and her initials eliminates all doubt. (A sample invoice and sketch are offered in chapter 12.)

Now, go over each room with its projection with the client. I usually say something like this: "Here's a breakdown of the rooms and their costs. Please look over each one and make sure I didn't leave anything out. I've included the flower over the light switch in your daughter's room at no extra charge since I feel it will add the perfect touch to her mural."

Give them a minute to check everything over. Here you should get some idea if your bid is too high or just right. Sometimes the client will blurt out, "Wow, these prices are really reasonable. This is great." Often, I hear, "Yup! Let's do it. It looks great!" (We say "Yup" in Colorado; you may hear "yessiree Bob," "ten-four," or a distinguished "you may proceed," depending on where you live!)

If the client merely looks over the invoice and says nothing, you're on! Try, "I've broken the job down by the room. You may want to start with one room now and add the others at a later date. I have clients who have me come back each summer after they receive their income tax refund." (This is usually met with a smile and a great deal of relaxation . . . you're not going to be one of those pushy salespeople.) Now the ball is in the clients' court. Give them a minute. Take this time to pull out your calendar and look for your next available opening. After a few moments, add, "Let me explain my procedure. I ask for half-down to reserve the date and cover my expenses. The balance is due upon completion, when you're thrilled and I'm packed up. I offer a free touch-up service, as I don't expect my clients to match the colors or techniques used. (If they have children, there will be a big smile here!) I guarantee the walls for as long as you have them. These are great paints. My next available opening is March 21st. Anytime after that I'm at your service. Now, may I answer any questions for you?"

You will get some feedback here. Either they will point out which rooms, if not all, they want to schedule you to do, or they'll ask questions. You can tell by the type of questions they ask if money is the concern, the dates offered, or if a spouse or second party has to be involved in the financial decision. If they tell you they can't give you an answer right now, be upbeat and tell them that you'll be happy to give them some time. Remind them, however, that you book clients on a first-come, first-serve basis and can't hold the date without a deposit. Keep this statement friendly and low-key. I usually add, "I just don't want you getting mad at me if you call in a day or two and I'm into April." Tell them to call with any questions and leave them with the top copy of the invoice. Take the other copy(ies) with you.

> **TIP:** If the client voices a concern about affording all of the job's bid, this is a perfect chance to bring up your referral program. Simply add that you have a way to bring in extra credit toward projects you've just discussed.

Here's a great way to introduce more ideas at the end of the interview without the client feeling any pressure to take them on now. Say something like, "Here's an idea for down the road if you're ever interested in something fun in here with these walls. By fauxing them in a soft denim blue, you'll not only reduce the starkness of the white walls but blue actually makes a wall recede visually, so the room will look bigger and more inviting at the same time. If you'd like, I can write down the estimate on the order we're doing today so that you'll have it if you decide to try this idea later."

This is such a low-pressure, non-threatening way to add to your order that nine times out of ten I hear, "Let's go ahead and do that. That would look great there!"

More often than not, you *will* land the bid at the first interview if you've covered everything we've talked about and you handle yourself with confidence and enthusiasm. Be attentive to their concerns and put the clients first. They'll feel it, and it will put you miles ahead of the competition.

If you sense the client can't afford the bid you've given, or they come right out and tell you they can't fit it in right now, you have an option if you really want the job. You can focus on *one* wall of the room as a focal point. Each room has a wall that is readily apparent as soon as you walk in. Usually a fireplace wall dominates a living or family room; bedrooms have a wall you glimpse first as you walk in, etc. With a beautiful faux finish or mural on just that one wall, the whole room will take on a new personality and assume some color and warmth. If it's a mural they are hesitating about, offer other choices. You don't have to paint the entire room in a wrap-around mural; bring in elements here and there instead. By losing the sky and wall-to-wall grass and simply painting hanging vines and animals here and there, you get the same effect without the cost. Some clients prefer this "open" feeling to a room completely surrounded in detail. Give them a few choices. If they still hesitate, let it go. Tell them to think it over and let you know. Add that you pride yourself on staying inside your client's budget and want them to be happy, not swallowing hard about your project. Thank them for their time and leave just as happy as you arrived!

Going Over the Contract

A complete contract is provided in chapter 10 along with other forms you'll find useful. The main consideration here is that everything is gone over in detail with the client to avoid any future miscommunications. Take the time here to answer questions and pencil in any concerns they—or you—want noted, due to special circumstances this project may require.

If working with a commercial client, fill in, in the appropriate blank, the times the company expects you to arrive and depart. List any special considerations the client wants noted on the contract. List the name of the foreman you will contact if working around new construction.

Whether residential or commercial, put down all important dates, locations for keys, locks, combinations, etc. If clients are offering to supply paint, repair walls, research photos, etc., write it down, and have them initial it. Under special requirements, list if you are to deal with pets. If a cat is strictly to remain indoors, you'll have to watch opening and closing doors. No stipulation is too small to list.

Please review the sample contract. Feel free to add your own specifications or wordage. Always have two copies: one for you and one for the client. Make sure both are signed and dated. A commercial job may require more copies, as foremen or board members may require their own.

The Deposit

When finalizing your bid, ask for half down to reserve your time and materials. When the check is submitted to you, write down the check number and "paid" next to the half-down figure on the invoice. Initial it. Tell the client you have listed her check number, amount, and that the deposit is covered. The top invoice is now given to her as her receipt for her records. Tell her the balance will be due upon completion.

A commercial client may have to write a PO (Purchase Order), and you will have to wait to receive your deposit. Note on the contract the terms and time period for receiving monies. Be specific concerning the date you need to have money in hand in order to proceed with purchase of materials and guarantee a starting date. Never settle for a "we'll get back to you." You are the other professional in this meeting and have rules *your* company runs by as well. Firmly stipulate your project demands and request a guaranteed date for payment, both for the deposit and balance. The commercial contract in chapter 10 covers everything to safeguard your rights as well as the clients'.

Occasionally you will have clients ask you to "hang on" to their deposit for a couple of days before depositing it. I don't have a problem with that. Tell them that you're happy to do so, but can only accommodate them for a few days, as this payment acts to reserve a date you'll be telling other prospective clients is taken. Call them the night before the requested deposit date and confirm that you may put it in your bank the following morning. Having a check bounce on you plays havoc with your account, so call ahead and make sure.

The same thing applies with clients who tell you they'll have to mail a deposit to you. Tell them you can't guarantee the date until payment is received. This discourages leaving the check sitting on their kitchen counter for several days before it finds its way to the mailbox. It also prevents clients from becoming angry over your giving their preferred dates to someone else. Always make the deposit policy clear. It will save you a fortune on aspirin.

6

IT'S TIME TO PAINT!

We've covered a good deal of information concerning walls and their finishes. Let's do a quick recap before we head for the job site.

Freshly Base-Painted Walls

If a repair job was done on any walls you'll be painting, or a new coat of paint added, a twenty-four-hour cure time must elapse before you begin. Paint dries from the outside, and, where the wall may feel dry to the touch, it can still be damp beneath the surface, causing damage to the surface as you manipulate paint during your faux work.

Wall Surfaces

Flat walls are harder to paint than textured walls and take longer. Why? Because they show every sponge and brush stroke and can look streaky. Flat walls require more coats of paint for mural work just to get them to look solid and vibrant. True, it's easier to do the outlining and detail work, but I'll take a knockdown wall any day. One advantage a flat wall has is in the patterned areas of faux, such as ragging, bagging, combing, *strie* (striping/dragging), etc.

Knockdown walls do not show the lovely patterns of some "imprint" fauxing. Combing is impossible. Taping off areas for gridwork, like that found in a faux stone, is also a pain on heavily textured walls. Orange-peel walls are great for both faux and murals. The surface has just enough texture to give it depth; you can use tape, and murals cover better, due to the lack of broken texture. Knockdown gives the prettiest results in faux leather, sponging, Old World glazes, and some marbling. Time and experience will help you bid the different walls. Just remember to add some time for flat—you'll thank me later. (One exception: If you are base-coating a wall first in a solid color, then doing a faux over it, flat will move faster than a texture, and if you are rendering today's new plaster textures, you will want a flat wall surface.)

Types of Service Paint

1. **Flat:** No sheen, poor durability, chalk-like finish that absorbs your paint, and you'll work twice as hard. You usually end up using a lot more paint. The poor, chalky, porous surface resists your sweeping movements with a sponge and results in a patchy-looking job.

   TIP: I mentioned in a previous chapter that I had a tip for working with a flat-painted wall surface. Try going to a semi-gloss or gloss paint instead of satin. The extra gloss element will help the glaze slide a little easier on a flat-painted surface. This idea was given to me by Lynn McNaul, and I am eternally grateful to her. Add a little more glazing medium as well to open up the drying time. The sheen will be "cut" by the dilution with water and glazing medium. Your local home center, paint, or hobby store also offers mediums that extend the open time of paint and will help it glide a little better over this dull sheen.

2. **Eggshell:** One step up from flat. Better "hide" (wall is sealed better than flat, and paint moves well on it). Low sheen. Fairly durable.
3. **Satin:** My favorite! Just enough sheen to add luster to the technique but not enough to draw the eye. Good durability and makes painting on top of it a breeze.
4. **Semi- and Gloss:** More sheen. Great for marbling, as you want a sheen for a faux marble surface. Most homeowners do not want a shiny wall, so avoid it for other techniques, except the tip mentioned above.

Always use professionalism in your painting. Avoid drips and curtaining. Clean, crisp edges and a good strong bond between paint coats are your goals. Clients will notice that white line at the top of the wall where the ceiling meets it, so make sure your paint goes all the way up.

Loading Up

Let's go to work. Load up all your supplies as neatly as possible. Entering a job site with wadded-up tarps, messy totes, and dripping cans is bad news. Try to compartmentalize your supplies for the different tasks you'll be doing. If you've installed a crate or plastic container in your car to hold your paint cans, load these tightly so they won't spill. (Your lids should be battened-down anyway!) Take only the paint you will need for the job; overloaded work areas in your vehicle will only make you stressful and will spill out into the street when you're pulling out ladders, etc. In chapter 12 I have included a checklist sheet that you can run off for each of your jobs. Check the items required for that day's work and load up.

Have only the items needed for the job loaded into your large tote. If you're using sponges that day, take these and the necessary tools, such as tape, measuring tape, pencils, glazing medium, etc. If you're stenciling, take along your stencil kit. I have a separate kit for my stenciling, as it is not one of the things I get asked to do as often as murals and faux, so it eliminates my having to haul around stencil supplies all the time. In the stencil kit are my stencil paints, creams, crayons, brushes, pencils, eraser, X-ACTO blades, adhesive spray, and level.

The goal here is to be organized and compact. Don't haul your entire studio into a job site when you're only needing a tray, bronze paint, and burnt umber.

Always carry your artist brushes in case you need a small liner brush to get into that half-inch crack between the doorjamb and the wall. You may need one to fill in a hairline gap where the ceiling meets the wall and your paint didn't quite get there.

Load up a bag with snacks, drinks, extra paper towels, music, etc. Healthy snacks such as nuts, fruit, or juices will give you extra energy at 10:00 A.M and 2:00 P.M., the two times of the day you might feel tired.

After you've loaded your paint cans, tarps, artist tote, buckets, and a bag of rags or paper towels, slide in your ladders. If you carry yours on a luggage rack, secure them with extra bungee cords or rope. Double-check your checklist. Your final note to self will be to check for fabric samples, pictures, books, or anything else you were supposed to bring to the job site. Have any items they loaned to you packed in as well.

> **TIP:** A couple of overlooked items I'm always leaving behind: a paint key to open the cans and a notepad and pencil to leave messages for the client or make notes for myself.

Arriving—On Time!

Pull up to the job site and ask the client before you begin unloading if where you've parked is convenient. Make sure all the furniture is out of the way before you begin bringing in your supplies. If the pictures are still on the wall and they've neglected to move all the furniture out of your way, sigh (to yourself) and begin helping the client empty the room, or at least the walls. If you have a lunch that needs refrigeration, ask if it's convenient to keep some things in their refrigerator. Ask where they would prefer you clean up and fill buckets with water. Now you're ready to move in the equipment.

Setup on Site

Bring in your tarps first, and cover the work-area floor. If there is furniture remaining, cover it with plastic or canvas drop cloths. Use painter's plastic rolls to cover mantels, bookcase tops, ledges, counters, etc., and tape it down. Tape off woodwork, baseboard, etc.

> **TIP:** Glazes are of a thinner consistency than full-strength paint and will seep under even the best-applied tape. I usually tape off only areas that are not straight-edged, such as curved mantel carvings, cornices, etc. I use a paint shield for everything else. This way, if paint seeps beneath the paint shield, I wipe it up immediately, and everything stays crisp and clean. If you wait until the end of the day to remove tape, you may be too late to remove seepage without using a strong paint remover. The paint shield also works great for getting up close to ceiling lines without taping off the entire area.

Use tarps with protective backs for carpeted areas; canvas ones will seep through if enough paint is spilled on them. Protect with drop cloths any areas you may be walking through on your way to and from the room to be painted. You might step in a paint drop on your tarp and track it somewhere else. The possibility of bringing in dirt, snow, or mud from outside will also require additional cloths leading to the work area.

Next, set up your work area. A small folding table saves your back and keeps paints up out of pets' and small children's reach. This also keeps you from stepping in a paint tray accidentally.

Now, bring in your ladders. Painters usually require four different ladders as part of their inventory: a sturdy eight-foot metal stepladder, a six-foot aluminum ladder, a small two-step ladder, and a sixteen-to-eighteen-foot extension ladder. Scaffolding is usually rented as needed, unless you'd like to invest in your own. The two largest ladders can be used with planks for stairways and other odd-angled jobs. There are also articulated ladders that bend into different configurations to allow for stairs or double as scaffolding. Extension devices can be bought to screw onto your extension ladder's legs that adjust to accommodate stairs. A new item on the market is a heavy-duty stair rung that snuggles up to the stair and allows you to place a ladder atop it. I love this thing! You can stand on it to stay level with the stair above it and it lifts easily from car to job site. Paint stores carry them.

> **TIP:** Never stand on the last rung at the top of a ladder. It will break or buckle due to the uneven distribution of weight. I know this from painful experience. Many years ago, I suddenly found myself sailing through the air and landing on my back in a paint tray after I attempted to get to those last two inches of space I couldn't quite reach on the ladder's top rung. If using an extension ladder on hardwood, tile, or linoleum floors, use a skid-proof kitchen mat beneath the bottom feet to keep it from sliding when you're up on it. This really works well!

Place your artist tote, buckets, and supplies on top of your folding table, or, if you don't use one, place them on the tarp in the center of the room where you won't be stepping over them as you paint the room's perimeter. As your sponge becomes clogged with paint, toss it into the bucket or when you need to break for a moment. Never leave sponges to dry full of paint. Buckets of water are also great for rinsing brushes, your hands, or tossing foam brushes into between finishes. This keeps your time going in and out of the kitchen or laundry room to a minimum.

Plug in your radio or CD player, unscrew your bottled water, and put on latex gloves, if you wear them. If you have set up a ladder by a closed door, someone may be coming through, so warn them now. Mix your paint, grab your tool of choice, and go to it!

> **TIP:** The same setup requirements will work on a commercial job site. You may be asked to keep your supplies in one contained area to eliminate blocking hallways or customer access. Always accommodate the client and don't complain. You may need to mix your paints and put the gallons back in your car, to cut down on the clutter. There are times when you may be moved around to accommodate patients or workmen . . . it's all part of the job when working with commercial projects, so try not to sweat it, and make good use of your time.

Keep sinks clean as you go! Whether residential or commercial, don't leave paint splattered all over the sink and back splashes. Wipe it up as you go. Other than the gorgeous walls you just painted, a client shouldn't know you've been there.

Project Tips

- Always mix a little more paint than you think you'll need. This will see you through in case of spills, a miscalculated area's needs, or touch-up paint saved for the client.
- You can bring disposable aluminum pans you buy at grocery stores (they are used for oven baking) to keep dripping paintbrushes and other tools in if you need to lay them down for a moment.
- Always have paper plates handy to use for murals and small paint jobs. I buy the compartmentalized plastic plates to use for small areas of paint. This frees you from carrying around heavy trays and a dozen cups.
- Kneepads are great and can save painful joints when doing floors or any wall you'll be kneeling in front of for long periods of time.
- Rubber pads designed to fit over the top poles of extension ladders are inexpensive and can save a wall from becoming scratched when you are leaning against the rungs. If you don't want to purchase pads, tie small towels or padded socks around the tops.

- Set paint cans in buckets and hang them with pothooks from your ladder, to lessen trips up and down the ladder and avoid spills. This works for painting a wall in a solid color. For glazes, mix them in a bucket about half-full and hook them to the ladder's rung.

- Take a small handheld vacuum with you on the job. There are usually sponge rubbings and dried paint flakes to clean up when you're through.

- Take a grocery bag or small trash bag to throw used paper towels into immediately, keeping your work area tidy and avoiding stepping onto wet, paint-soaked towels. This also keeps kitty from finding a new chew toy.

- When working on an entire room, always work from left to right, starting in the upper left-hand corner. If you're left-handed, you may want to reverse this tip. When painting up against an adjacent wall, keep the paint only on the wall you're painting and don't go around the corner onto the unpainted wall. It will dry into a line before you can get back to that wall. Either tape it off or do what I do: hold the paint shield tightly into the corner as you go to keep the glaze *only* on the wall you're painting. If you anticipate stopping for any reason, try and finish a wall, as it will show where you stopped if you're working with most glazing techniques.

- Keep a wet paper towel with you at all times. Use this to "feather out" the edges of glaze, if you're worried about a fast drying time. Glazes will leave a dark edge wherever you stop, and feathering these out with a wet paper towel leaves you with a soft, uneven area to continue working around.

- Always work top to bottom, not side to side with glazes. Side-to-side motions leave a horizontal line, whereas top to bottom, done in a jagged pattern, won't draw the eye when it dries. I try to move in and out as I glaze downward from the ceiling, creating a pattern that looks like jigsaw pieces. This way there is no vertical line to draw the eye.

- Step back often to view your work. Once a glaze dries, you are left with few options to fix dark areas or drips and runs. Usually your only recourse is to paint over it with the base paint and start over.

- If you are fauxing over light-switch plates, remove them from the wall and paint them separately on a newspaper or drop cloth. Painting them while they are on the wall usually leaves a dark area around them where you tried to work the paint, and puddles can accumulate beneath them and run, just about the time your back is turned and you've moved on to another area of the wall. Coat them with a water-based acrylic low-sheen sealant, as outlets and plates receive a lot of poking and scratches.

- Wipe off ceiling swipes, baseboard bleeds, and any other paint "boo-boos" immediately, before they dry. If the client will be gone while you are working, ask them before they leave if they have the base paint used for the wall in case you have any bleeds to deal with. (Bleeds are paint that seep beneath your shield or tape.)

- Step back across the room to ensure you covered areas above doorways and windows. Sometimes you'll leave a bare spot where you thought you had taken the paint all the way to the trim work.

- Tape dangling window-covering pulls to the window, to keep them out of your way and protect them from paint.

- Keep Ziploc plastic bags with you to encase brushes, sponges, and rollers in until you get back to your studio and do a *proper* cleanup of them.

- And as I've mentioned earlier, my new favorite artist's companion is a 3-drawer plastic cart on wheels. You can find these at Walmart for $10. They roll right along with you, offer a flat top on which you can place reference material, paints, etc., and they keep everything off the floor and out of the way when contained within the three see-through drawers. I keep items like my pencils, erasers, snacks, business cards, a notepad, X-Acto blades, tapes, measuring devices, paint key, and folding paint brush holder in the top drawer. In the second drawer I put my acrylic tubes of paints. The bottom drawer holds spackle, sandpaper, paper towels, small palettes, solvents, and extra cans of paint. I will also have small children's books or inexpensive toys I pick up from Dollar Stores in the cart to award to someone who has been helpful or is perhaps having a bad day. Again, ask before handing a child anything, even a book. If you want the book back, ask the child to please return it when he/she has finished with it.

- Take along a folding chair if you don't like sitting on a small step ladder.

Commercial Jobs

Project tips for commercial jobs are basically the same, with a few exceptions:

- Ask, when you arrive, where the most convenient place would be to keep the supplies you're not using immediately. You may be directed to a broom closet, an area beneath the receptionist's counter, or the bathroom.
- Bring in only the things you'll need for the job. If you're glazing a wall, bring in the paint, technique tool, tray, tarps, ladder, and shield.
- Mix the paint ahead of time at your studio, if you can. Add your glazing mediums and water (or whatever additive you're working with), and transport it in a new paint can or bucket. This keeps you out of the way on the commercial site and saves you from hogging the sinks in the public bathroom or a lab area.
- Leave the music at home if you're working on a site where they are open for business.
- Never interrupt a businessperson while he is dealing with customers or patients. Ask the receptionist or another person who is unoccupied at the moment to relay to the owner a message that you need to ask him a question when he has a minute.
- Don't park in parking places reserved for the staff or customers. Pull into a loading zone area, if they have one, and quickly unpack what you'll need, then move to another parking area.
- Keep your equipment and supplies well out of the way of walk-throughs and door accesses.
- Eat lunch in your car or an area where clientele won't be in the vicinity.

- Address owners, doctors, and other professionals by the name they use at work, even if you know them as, say, Charles. Calling Doctor Wilson by his nickname, Chuck, probably won't sit well with him in front of his constituents.
- If you borrow a pencil, pen, or pad of paper, put it back.
- Make sure you have an adequate supply of paper towels, cups, etc., so as not to borrow from the business. This becomes annoying to personnel.
- Keep the friendly banter to a minimum. The people around you are here to work. Let them take the lead as to how much conversation they are interested in. Don't ask personal questions of patients or others you might happen to overhear speaking of problems. Bottom line: You're there to paint the walls, not entertain the troops.
- Be respectful of others in their work areas. Secretaries, nurses, and waitresses were not asked if they wanted the walls painted, and they may see you as nothing but an interruption. Apologize for the inconvenience and work around their schedules and areas as quickly and quietly as possible. A little courtesy goes a long way here.
- Take along your own folding chair if you'll need one for murals or half-walls. Borrowing company chairs, or residential ones, is frowned upon. After all, you're *painting*. No one wants to worry about paint getting onto their furnishings.
- Tell the owner ahead of time that it would be a good idea to open windows to ventilate the area. If it is cold outside, bring in a small fan.
- Take stretching breaks and go outside occasionally to get some fresh air.

The final word, whether you are working with commercial clients or residential, is to go easy on yourself! I am usually "wiped out" when I get home from a project, due to tired muscles, eyes, and brain cells. I put a lot of pressure on myself to turn out a perfect project every time, and that can take a toll on you. The creative process is tiring. So give yourself a break. Do your very best but don't become your own worst enemy by *stressing* about every detail.

Dealing with Contractors

We've covered a good deal of information on contractors in previous chapters. I would like to add here that my working relationships with outside contractors have been wonderful. With very few exceptions, these people are courteous, helpful, and a great deal of fun to be around. They have offered to carry my ladders, opened doors for me, and shared doughnuts.

The information I want to pass on in this section is this: treat them as the trained professionals they are. Compliment their work, and it will go a long way. You are what I call a "spotlight" talent. The decorative artists get all the "oohs and aahs," and sometimes that takes a toll on the guy working next to you wiring a ceiling or working on the trim. Murals are especially guilty of receiving overwhelming praise. Most clients are only looking for the mistakes the contractors working around you are making and very seldom give them a kind word, let alone break into a chorus of thank-yous! Therefore, I go the extra mile to let these talented people know that I think what they do is interesting and takes a lot of skill. It is heartfelt and not at all manipulative. Let me give you an example:

Several years ago, I was referred to owners of a large home who wanted a good deal of faux work and murals done. The builder had also commissioned his interior painter to be there to paint the entire house in a soft, sage green. The painter and his crew were there every day, and no matter what I did to get on his good side, he treated me with indifference and, at times, rudeness. I finally decided to just go about my business. One day, while painting an area over his sage-green base coat, I heard him mutter to his crew, "Sure, she paints over my hard work *and* she gets the big bucks!"

I was surprised and a little hurt. Rather than ignore it, since he worked for a builder who often referred me to jobs, and I was pretty sure I'd run into him again, I got down off the ladder and approached him. In front of his crew, I said, "I happen to think that what you do is harder than what I do. To 'straight-paint' walls takes more time and is harder than some of the glazes I work with. Your base coat is what's giving this particular technique its depth, and I appreciate your detail and quality of work. You must be good, or this particular builder wouldn't use you exclusively on his homes. I hope we can work together, because I hope to be referred often by this company."

He sniffed a few times, glanced at his coworkers, and mumbled a "yeah, okay." I went on with my work and noticed a slight change: the rudeness turned into witty jabs and outright sarcasm. Since I pride myself on being able to sling a few witticisms myself, I gave as good as I got. We ran into each other on many sites after that, and the banter continued. We had his crew and everyone else around us laughing whenever we were in the same room together.

One particular day, he was in rare form and nailed me every time he came around the corner, with remarks such as "If you drip on my perfect walls, you get to clean it up," and "I don't know why they pay you the big bucks; I could splash paint across the wall with a kitchen rag in my sleep!" On that day, I had just finished a large aquatic mural in the child's room of the house

and was backing up to take a picture of it. He and his crew came around the corner just as the camera flash went off. "Ow, I'm blind!" he screamed dramatically. I turned, smiled, and said, "Well, that explains your work!" We have been best friends ever since.

Give the contractors you work with respect and try to work out your scheduling with theirs. It was not their idea to have all of you bunched in there together on a project at the same time. They usually answer to a boss; you don't, so they may be a little tense about a certain timeline. Work out the pecking order in the parking lot so that everyone isn't fighting for the best spot near the entrance. Remember: you will likely run into these people on future job sites. Take their cards. I am always running into clients wanting to know if I know anyone who wires, tiles, does trim work, etc. They often take my cards, and referrals have resulted from it. Besides, when you're working around other artisans, the spotlight isn't tilted fully on you *all* the time. The owner will be talking with these workers off and on, and you'll get a little quiet time.

7

THE FINISHING TOUCH

Working with several personalities in one month can be like juggling balls with different faces painted on them. Some of those faces will be smiling, some scowling, and some indifferent. Clients come with an assortment of quirks and idiosyncrasies. Your job is to feel them out in the beginning and get a grasp of what you'll be working with . . . and then thrill them! It sounds like a big order because it is. Dealing with the public is trying: they'll have bad days, just like you, and you'll wonder if they're unhappy because of your work or because the lightning storm the night before took out their television reception.

Leaving the Customer Thrilled!

I have a way of getting through the days when I am not particularly thrilled to be working around a certain client. Rather than stew about it and predict how awful the day is going to be, I stop and really think about the client for a moment and surround them in my mind with kind thoughts. I go out the door determined to make them happy and treat their project as if it were my own. It is amazing how well this attitude change affects my day and the client's mood. They sense when I come in that I care about the job they hired me to do, and the day ends so much better than I thought it would.

This may sound Pollyanna to you, but let me explain something: the measure of success I've obtained in this career is due primarily to my customer-relations skills. I truly care about those people who have dipped into their savings and entrusted me with their hard-earned income . . . and their home or business. I cannot count how many homes I have been in where they didn't have furniture in the front room or a dining table, but they were paying me $700 to turn their child's room into a fantasy place.

Leaving the customer thrilled has a lot to do with your attitude toward their project and your appreciation of their choosing you to do it. Most clients get several bids before deciding, especially if you're new to the business. Once you've established a reputation, you won't go through the bidding process as much. Be grateful for the work and then go out and knock their socks off. Here're some "guaranteed thrillers":

- Show up on time.
- Ask how things are going with them. Are the kids excited for Christmas, how did the trade show go, are they going nuts planning their daughter's wedding? Show some interest before you start painting and then get to work.
- Treat their home or business as if it were your own. Take care of an "ugly spot" or white line along the ceiling before *they* mention it. If you need to take an extra hour to make an area look right because you miscalculated the technique, then do it. You won't get referrals over sloppy or half-hearted work.
- Learn their children's names and use them. The same with pets. Never show disgust over an owner's pet, even if you think cats are evil. If you need to have a pet removed from the area, tell the owner it's for the pet's safety, not that the poor creature is bugging you.
- Never look in their cabinets, without asking, for drinking glasses, pencils, or anything else you forgot to bring with you.
- Ask before using their bathroom, and leave it spotless.
- When placing paint cans, equipment, or buckets on kitchen counters or furniture tops, always put a protective tarp down first. Owners are very particular about their expensive counter surfaces. Always tape off trim work, splash tiles, and cabinets.
- Work around the owners' schedule without complaint. If they don't want to have you around at 7:30 A.M. while they're trying to get their kids off to school, then accommodate them.

- Don't place your lunch or drinks in their refrigerator without asking.
- Make sure you're not blocking the driveway or street access.
- If you smoke, go outside by your vehicle, and then remove any butts.
- Some new commercial sites will have an ant problem while construction is going on. Never leave food wrappers on the premises. Take empty soda cans, all food, wrappers, crumbs, etc., with you when you leave. I learned this the hard way when I left a bag of chips in my art kit overnight and returned the next day to find an army of ants surrounding my things.
- At the end of the day, pack all your things into your car, or, if already arranged with the client, in some specific area, such as a garage or laundry room.
- At the end of the project, go over every inch of baseboard, trim, mantel tops, bookcase tops, etc., and look for small paint splatters Always find the mistakes before the client does.
- Bring an adequate supply of paper towels, pencils, etc., so you're not borrowing things from the client. If you do need to use something, replace it before the job ends.
- Never, under any circumstances, use vulgar language. If the owner swears like a Caribbean sailor and you're tempted to join in, resist the urge and maintain your professional status.
- If the client leaves before you do, ask if you are to lock the door behind you when you leave. Don't assume on this one. I have locked doors only to find they had no key and it was their only way into the house!
- Ask clients if they'd like you to accept packages while they're away or if they prefer you not answer the door.
- If you're painting around plug-ins, gain permission to unplug computers, answering machines, phones, etc. before doing it. This could lead to huge problems if you don't ask ahead of time.
- If your client will be away from the project, ask for a way to reach her in case you have an emergency or a question arises concerning the job.

- Replace any knickknacks, hanging pictures, furniture, etc., when you're through, if you're so inclined. I usually do this to surprise clients who will be returning home after a hard day at work. It's a nice feeling to walk into an organized room that looked like a war zone when they left for work earlier.
- Tape off phone, computer, and television plugs, so they don't get paint on them if you are leaving any of these plugged into the wall.
- Double check faucets, sink handles, and sink areas for paint before you quit for the day.
- When painting bathrooms, neatly lay in another room their towels, throw rugs, tank covers, and anything else that's in your way, to avoid dripping on these items.
- Never have a friend drop by to see you while you're on the job! This is unprofessional, and homeowners especially will feel violated to have strangers in their home.
- Keep personal calls to a minimum, and bring your own phone.

My final finishing touch is to leave the client with a thank-you gift of some kind. This is usually something I've picked out to emphasize the theme of the room we just finished. For instance, if I were hired to paint a room with fake windows looking out onto the ocean with a lighthouse and dolphins, I would buy a small lighthouse statuette from a gift shop or hobby store. An Italian-kitchen faux finish might inspire the purchase of a fancy oil-and-vinegar bottle, or a salad-bowl set.

The price and nature of the gift are usually related to the price of the project. Obviously, if you just finished a $10,000 job and literally faux-finished the entire first floor of the clients' home, a gift certificate to a pricey restaurant or a weekend getaway to the nearest ski resort might be a more appropriate gift.

If you are dealing with a commercial client, a plant for the office or a gift certificate to a local restaurant often works well if you're concentrating on one person. If, however, you are involved with a number of people at a certain place of business, you could try this.

Recently, I finished work on a large remodel of a medical clinic where construction workers and the staff at the medical facility were all involved.

The day before my deadline, my husband and I brought in lunch for everyone. From a glazed ham with side dishes, right down to the doughnuts, we let all the people involved know how much we appreciated their business and their help on the project. It was very much appreciated and a great way to end on a high note.

Include a thank-you card. If it's one you make on your computer with a personalized theme reflecting the job you just finished, so much the better. Have fun with it.

Finally, surprise clients with the unexpected. Throw in a butterfly over the light switch in their daughter's room where you just finished an elaborate garden scene. Add another vine climbing over a cabinet if you feel it's just the right touch to make the project sparkle. If it would take you ten to thirty minutes to add some extra touch that would make the room sing, do it. It's that simple going-the-extra-mile that will stay in the clients' memory and have them singing your praises to their neighbors.

Future Business

In a world where customer service becomes more of a rarity every year, the professional who offers it truly stands out. I'm sure you've noticed stores where the cashiers are more friendly and helpful than what you're used to. My husband and I comment on it all the time. It is evident the store policy hammers customer service in their sales meetings. Even the smiling face at a drive-thru window stays with you and shines in comparison to the scowling countenance of the next employee you run into.

Your future business in this career depends on your personality as well as your talent. Be consistent in your pleasant, upbeat attitude, and your clients will find themselves looking forward to having you around. A huge percentage of my friends started out as clients. It's one of the greatest perks of this job.

When you finish a job and have discreetly left your thank-you gift and card, leave a few business cards or flyers with it. If the owner is on the premises, remind him of your referral program and thank him ahead of time for mentioning your name. As I said earlier, I usually add something like, "It's my clients' kind referrals that have kept me out of the Yellow Pages for the past five years now. I really appreciate it."

If the client mentions wanting some more work done in the future, say, "I'm ready when you are. I tell you what . . . if it looks like I'm getting booked well into fall, I'll call you and see if you want to get in my scheduling book before we're into Christmas!" Leave it light and nonpressuring.

This truly is the best part of the business: seeing your clientele grow because you took such good care of them and surpassed their expectations.

8

EXPANDING: WHEN YOU'RE TOO SUCCESSFUL

Don't you love this title? It's a great feeling to know you have the tools in your hands to become *too* successful. By applying the information imparted throughout this book, you can bring the reality of a booming business well within reach.

There will come a time in your career when you may want to hang up the one-man art kit and consider bringing others onboard. For me, that decision came when I couldn't keep up with the orders but didn't really want to bring in a partner. For you, it could happen right from the beginning; you may want someone to share the responsibilities with.

Take a moment now and decide just how big you want your business to grow. Do you envision working out of your home forever, controlling the amount of work you take on and possibly turning a few jobs down when the pressure sets in? Perhaps your goal is to become part of a successful interior decorating firm, acting as their in-house artist. Many decorators do have their own faux-finishing staff onboard.

Very few artists require a retail space, as one normally meets with clients in their home or place of business. Retail outlets are used by decorators carrying a line of product such as mini-blinds, carpet, etc. If you feel a private office setup somewhere would help separate your work life from your family life, by all means, rent some quiet little space with a storage area for paints, ladders, and the rest of your supplies.

In the next section, we will take a look at bringing on others for your business. For now, take a good hard look at how much freedom you want to relinquish when you take on a staff, whether they are freelance or full-time employees.

Subcontracting or Freelance Artists

When you decide to involve other artists in your business, things change. Some of those changes are for the better, and some bring on a new set of headaches. Instead of controlling every situation involving your hard-won clientele, you are now handing some of the decisions and outcome to someone else.

The first time I hired a freelance artist to work with me, I envisioned more freedom for myself. Surely, this was a good thing; two people to turn out the work, getting some space opened up on my calendar so I could breathe a little between jobs.

Then reality hit! It started with a phone call from the client telling me my artist had not shown up for work. Two days later, when she did show up, I was called because the faux finish was not up to the client's expectations. When I went over to see for myself, I was appalled. It was awful. What happened to the talent who rendered those wonderful sample boards I had been shown when I interviewed this person? I took her aside and pointed out the areas that would have to be redone. After three attempts to correct it, the artist panicked and quit. I was now left with my workload and hers. I stormed into my home and told my husband I would eat dirt before hiring anyone else again.

Eight months down the road, I caved when, once again, I had too much work, and these wonderful artists came along. This time I insisted on seeing walls they had actually painted, and was impressed. Their personalities were upbeat; they dressed nicely. So with high hopes I hired them for three projects. On the first project, a light fixture was broken; on the second, it was a ceiling fan; and on the final job, they spilled paint from a ledge down the kitchen cabinets and onto the countertops. I was called in to fix all three projects.

To date, I am working alone and much happier. I do have the phone numbers of several talented people in my Rolodex, but I use them with one stipulation: they are on their own. I will refer them to a client with the understanding that I am no longer in the picture. If mistakes are made, it is up to them to fix them. I tell the client ahead of time that I am unable to schedule her project but know of a talented person who might be able to do it. I then tell the client I am not responsible for the project's outcome. I am referring this person due to his talent and reputation for quality work, but the client will be hiring an individual, not my business name. For these referrals, I usually receive a 10 percent commission and am happy to give these talented people business; I've just learned the hard way that I'm happier keeping the control over my projects.

If you do take on freelance artists or subcontract work out to anyone, whether they are construction workers or interior decorators, put in writing what the job entails and who is responsible for which aspects of it. Clearly spell out the dates, deadlines, and time requirements. Make sure freelancers have the appropriate insurance coverage for the job. Go over parking limitations, client preferences, and penalties should their portion of the project go over the deadline or incur any problems.

Make sure the client has a copy of the agreement and knows which part of the job relates solely to you and which areas do not involve you. Break down the pay scale and make sure all the workers involved understand the terms of payment and the date they will be paid. Now, have everyone initial and sign it.

Too often, a person you've brought onboard for a certain project runs into money problems and calls you asking for an advance or payment due on completion when you have not yet been paid for the job. Having a date for payment, that he has initialed, will help tremendously with this problem. Never pay workers before you receive payment. A problem may arise with their portion of the project and, once paid, they may make excuses or procrastinate taking care of it.

Even if the job is a small one, put all the details in writing and have subcontractors sign it. You don't need the headache of dealing with the little things if something goes wrong.

Whenever possible, compartmentalize the job into each subcontractors section, i.e., the artist you brought in to add brick work to your Italian kitchen will have a separate bid price and deadline; the masonry contractor putting in expensive tiled countertops will have his own breakdown of costs, dates, and payment. This way, if they are behind, or the project demands change in their area but not yours, you won't be penalized on your payment or brought into the discussion of their work division.

This may sound like having freelance employees is a headache. Not always. I'm on the other end of the stick as well, and enjoy the relationship I have with people who freelance work out to me. I'm sure they worry about whether or not I'll have any problems on the job site of a client they were kind enough to refer me to.

A few pointers when interviewing for freelance help:

- Take your time in the interview and find out what their work ethics are. If they appear too laid-back, even lazy, then pass.
- What are their personalities like? Do they have good eye contact or are they extremely nervous? Is their body language stiff and withdrawn?
- How are their grammar and people skills? Do they seem confident?
- How are they dressed? If they've shown up for an important interview dressed in dirty jeans and a wrinkled shirt, imagine what they'll wear to paint a house!
- How is their hygiene? This is important; a client will remember offensive body odors long after the job is completed.
- As they show you their work, are they enthusiastic or mumbling? Do they make a lot of excuses for their samples or photos? This presentation they are showing you now will be the same one proffered to a client. Would you hire this person if you were the client?
- Are their photos and samples clean and well organized, or stuffed into a shoebox?

Make sure, when you hire freelancers or subcontractors, whether on a temporary basis or for the long run, that you understand they represent your company when they are out in the world. Unless you've notified the client ahead of time that this person is not working under your umbrella but rather an independent businessperson whom you're referring for this particular project, you take on this new artist's problems if he should fall short in any area . . . from the interview to the finished project.

One last word of caution when dealing with freelancers or subcontractors: don't let them in on details of future projects you're bidding on. They just might beat you to the punch and recruit the job for themselves. Avoid bragging about future work or giving out client names. I learned the hard way that when someone is hungry for work, you become last on the list of considerations. Keep your private life private, and be very cautious about letting these people know the details of your business.

If you're careful during the interview process and build a solid foundation with them, freelance artists can become a good thing. Many wonderful work relationships have been built. It may take a few trial-and-error start-ups before you find the right combination. That's okay. Most great relationships do.

Your subcontractors and freelance artists are not employees of your business; they work for themselves. These independent contractors should provide you with a Social Security number (SSN) or employer identification number (EIN). Ask these contractors to sign Form W-9 before they begin work for you.

If you are using subcontractors or freelance artists, and they've earned more than $600 while working for you, you must file Form 1099-MISC. This form will go to the IRS as well as a copy to the contractor for his filing purposes.

A Whole New Ball Game

If you've reached the point where you would like to bring in help on a more permanent basis, then it's time to consider hiring employees. This comes with more paperwork and tax obligations.

Withholding FIT

Your new employees will fill out a W-4 Form that claims the number of withholding allowances. Use IRS Publication 15 or Circular E to determine the appropriate amount of federal income tax to withhold.

Withholding FICA

You will withhold Social Security and Medicare taxes from your employees' paychecks. The percentages these withhold are 6.2 percent for Social Security for wages up to $65,400 and 1.45 percent for Medicare.

FUTA Tax

FUTA is your unemployment tax. You will pay 6.2 percent of your employee's first $7,000 in earnings. This tax return is filed once a year using Form 940, or 940-EZ. This is different from your other filings as the form is due January 31. Your state will have unemployment tax, and you'll receive credit from the federal government for the state payment.

Form 941

Yes, more forms. Are you sure you want to bring in employees? This one has to do with employee compensation and taxes withheld along with your employer's share of FICA. Use Form 941: Employer's Quarterly Federal Tax Return.

Forms W-2 and W-3

Form W-2 sums up an employee's income and withholding for one year. Your artists must receive copies of these forms no later than January 31. In addition, you must attach the form(s) to Form W-3 and send it happily along to the Social Security Administration.

Corporation Structures

If you've set your business up as a corporation instead of a sole proprietorship or partnership, the taxes fall differently. Form 1120 is required for corporate income taxes on net profits. Corporate tax rates can range between 15 percent to 30 percent of the businesses' profits.

Corporations also pay for the employees' Social Security and Medicare tax.

Employer Identification Number

Your employer identification number (EIN) must be applied for if you have employees under you. To apply for this number, use Form SS-4. Whereas you could get by with your Social Security number for identification purposes while running your business as a sole proprietor, you must now meet government regulations by obtaining an EIN and file quarterly employment taxes using Form 8109.

You will receive federal tax deposit coupons when you apply for your EIN. Again, use IRS Publication 505: Estimated Tax Payments and Form

1040-ES' Estimated Tax Worksheet to figure how much tax you're likely to pay.

If any of this sounds confusing, consult your local government regulations or hire a good tax accountant to help you get started. Having an accountant help with your business is a good idea anyway when you've reached the point of hiring employees.

Paying Your Employees

At this point you will also have to decide payment arrangements with your full-time help. A career in the arts differs from most other professions, as each day and each project is different in its needs and payment. Setting up a predetermined salary would be difficult if not impossible.

If you feel that setting a payment ceiling is the only way you could keep organized books in your business, go ahead. Figure out a pay schedule based on an hourly rate that you and your artist are comfortable with: say, $50 an hour. He logs in and out at the end of the day, and his amount of hours worked is duly recorded.

Perhaps a flat-rate system makes more sense. The artist is paid on a daily basis rather than hourly: for instance, $400 a day. If the bid for a certain job was $1,200, you would deduct your percentage for your company's overhead and decide if your artist could feasibly finish the job at $400 a day within the given time frame.

If your company percentage is 15 percent to cover business expenses, and you subtract this from the $1,200, it would leave you with $960. Now, if you withhold an additional 10 percent commission for yourself (it is *your* business, after all), you would subtract an additional $96 from the project price. The new amount to be earned for this project is $864. If you are paying your employee $400 a day, he will have to turn out this project in a little over two days. Can he do it? What happens if there are complications?

The more sensible solution is to take a bid, deduct your company percentage of 15 percent and your personal commission of 10 percent, and tell the artist the amount he will earn for rendering that particular project. If it takes him longer than he thought, then the two of you may have to come up with an escalated bidding process, or he'll have to work faster.

My personal problem with having others work for me was a feeling of losing control over the project once someone else showed up to do the work I bid on. I insisted on doing the bids myself, then informed my freelance artists how much the job would pay after going over the project with them. If your employees are slower, or not as efficient as you would like them to be, this can cause problems with the client. Here again, you will have to find the cream of the crop when hiring artists to work for you.

What about Office Space?

Having a home-based business has many advantages. The commute time can be the five minutes you spend going from your bedroom to your office in the basement. The demands on your wardrobe are minimal; just some nice clothes for interviews and your painting wardrobe. Running an office could require an investment in additional business attire.

The obvious advantage is the low overhead: the amount you're paying to live in your home already. Taking on office space will require rent, utility, water, and other facility fees. You may have to park away from the entrance if the parking spaces are reserved for clientele.

Having an office can eliminate the pressures of home life. Keeping family and work separate is very important to some people; and some finally tire of telling everyone to stay off the phone or having to vacuum because a client is dropping by some samples. An office can afford a professional setting or a showroom for fauxed walls or vignettes displaying your murals.

The problem with this scenario is that your business almost always takes place at the clients' address. You have to see their walls, carpets, fabrics, etc., in order to offer color solutions and bid the area. Clients rarely come to your place of employment unless it's to go over blueprints for a building not yet under construction or to drop off payments, fabric, tile samples, or books with illustrations of the mural work they'd like to have emulated. Your supplies require little space unless you get into heavy equipment, such as scaffolding, generators, and numerous ladders.

To be honest, I don't know of any faux painters or muralists working out of an office setup. Your dreams might incorporate one. Take a close look at the financial requirements involved in using office space, and if that's where your heart is, go for it!

9

THE WONDERFUL WORLD OF MURALS

I actually got my start in this business painting wall murals, and then branched out into faux finishing when it hit the artist's market. People assumed if you were painting murals, you probably could render faux finishes. When I realized the popularity and beauty of glazed walls, I dove in and discovered I was still using water-based paints for the most part, and my knowledge of color and artist's tools served me well. But it was the murals that still thrilled me and received the most attention.

The amazing thing about murals is that you can paint them anywhere a blank space is found. You will see them on the sides of buildings, on vehicle bodies, boats, mud flaps, bathrooms, ceilings, sidewalks, garden walls, kitchens, nurseries, pots, pans, and saw blades. With an arena like that, how can you not succeed to some measure in this career? Clients have brought me milk cans, tire covers, fireplace screens, old signs, desks, dressers, and, more recently, an expensive doll resembling the client's daughter . . . with one exception: the manufacturer left off the freckles.

In chapter 3 we covered a plethora of ideas for finding customers in the faux and mural business. We won't repeat that information here. Whether you are looking for faux work or mural work, you will seek clients using the same advertising techniques. Door-to-door flyers work extremely well with murals, as you can target homes with outdoor play equipment if you're interested in doing children's murals. Often, just getting in the door for a child's room can lead to bids for other rooms in the house once they've seen your portfolio and realize the potential for the bare walls in the rest of the home. Sadly, a good majority of the population equate murals with children's rooms unless they happen to see one in a home show. So don't be shy in educating them about the Wonderful World of Murals!

Bidding Murals Is Different

When a muralist does sketches for clients, they are called thumbnails or maquettes. Their purpose is to give an overview of the completed project. While the more accuracy and detail you can include is helpful in conveying your vision, it is very time consuming. Also, with more detail you have less room for confusion. With murals, you will often be asked to add a few more elements. If the sketch is very precise in what is being offered for the agreed upon price, the client cannot say things such as, "Oh, I thought there might be more boats in this scene," or, "I think another horse would round this area out instead of just the one in the foreground." This way you can refer to the sketch and point out what was agreed upon and offer to add more for an additional charge. I also write out a thorough overview of characters, elements, and other details on the proposal. For instance in a child's room recently, I did a rough sketch and on the companion proposal put:

1. Three rabbits near picket fence gate
2. Garden shed with one hoe, small rake, and gardener's hat on the west side of building
3. Green meadows with clusters of yellow, red, and white flowers on left side of mural only
4. Picnic blanket under oak tree...no items requested to be on blanket
5. Picket fence to run the length of the wall with one open gate at center
6. No people are requested or other animals, birds, butterflies, etc.
7. Sky will be blue with white fluffy clouds. No sun is visible. Clouds will correspond to the number shown in the sketch.

As you can see, I get as detailed as possible, thanks to past experience. Describe the mural with enthusiasm and in great detail, using your hands to show how large things will appear on the wall. When someone says a small rabbit, they might be thinking 3' tall on the wall. By using your hands to show proportions, or a yardstick, you can get a quick feel for how large they are thinking the elements will be.

Finally, do not do mural samples and sketches for free if they want to see them before offering you the job. Charge a small fee, such as $30, or however much you feel your time is worth. If I have the job and am merely cementing down the theme and detail, then I include sketches with the purchase price. If they make repeated changes to the sketches and you are sure you understood their original intent, you may need to tell them that additional changes will incur a small artist's fee. Some people don't realize the time it takes to make additions, changes, and deletions.

When you are estimating a mural job, it is imperative that you study the wall's texture carefully. In faux finishing, the wall's finish determines which technique would work best on it and which glaze would not work at all; with murals, the texture does much more.

Murals are detailed works of art and require tiny liner brushes for the fine outlining and highlights. If you are faced with a heavily troweled wall or one with deep pockets of knockdown texturing, you will have to bid more to compensate for the extra time involved in creating a consistent and pleasing composition. Outlining or fine brush strokes for, say, animal hair, is extremely difficult over ridges and pits.

The walls' paint finish will again come into play, as a flat wall paint base will slow you down and absorb your paint. You will need to bid for additional time and materials. A high-gloss paint can also be a nightmare, as it can repel water-based paints, such as acrylics, and you will have to clean it first with denatured alcohol to kill the sheen or do a light sanding to create a fine tooth that will accept your paints. Eggshell or satin are your best bets for a perfect base to paint upon. If you will be painting a new home which is now under construction, request that the area(s) for the mural work is base-coated in satin.

Another consideration for murals when bidding, which doesn't impact the estimating for faux, is the placement of doors, windows, and obstructions. In faux painting, these areas factor in only in determining how long the room will take to glaze. With murals, every element that intrudes into a wall area becomes an obstacle to deal with in terms of how it breaks up the illusion. That window on the east wall . . . do we create a mural with a window at just that location, going for a trompe l'oeil effect, or ignore it and paint our mural around it? (Trompe l'oeil is French, and it means to "trick the eye.")

You may be painting walls in a restaurant and have to paint around ductwork, plumbing, grill hoods, and booths. Will the mural suffer for these intrusions, or do you paint over them so that they become part of the mural?

With murals, the room architecture will dictate the layout and design of the artwork. You cannot give a ballpark bid over the phone without seeing the walls you are asked to estimate. Closet doors can play a major role in your mural, and their placement will determine the room's design. Ceiling fixtures must be taken into consideration, as well as floors (are they carpet or wood?) and soffits.

"Eyeballing" the Room

There is only one way to bid a mural, in my opinion, and that is the flat-rate or "eyeballing" estimate.

It would be impossible to apply the square-foot rule here, as it would be impossible to apply an hourly rate; too many things factor into creating a mural to put it on the clock. Walking into the room and living with it for a moment is the only way to bid a mural job.

Each room is different. The angle of the wall; the direction the windows face, affecting the room's light; the position of the doors, windows, closets, cabinets, fireplace, etc., all impact a mural's design and composition. Whether the mural will have a horizontal layout or vertical one will be determined by the wall's height as well as where it falls. If the area a client wants painted is flanked by two doors, giving the wall a decided vertical balance, then choosing a sweeping landscape would be a mistake. Tall poplars with a hint of scenery would, however, lend itself to the wall's composition.

If the client has her heart set on a fake window in the guest powder room, but the room already has several windows or one dominating one, then another window might look odd or overworked. You may have to lead her in a different direction. Sometimes a client will want a massive mural in a room so small that the artwork would overwhelm it. Few clients are what I call visual, and you will have to tactfully help them determine the appropriate scale for the room.

A theme that pops up frequently is the one where a client has seen a breathtaking mural at a Parade of Homes and wants one rendered in the same way in the same room of their home. The downside of this fantasy is that the room they're hoping to duplicate seldom resembles the one in the show home. Usually they are hoping to have you cram the same masterpiece into an area half the size. Here's where your people skills come in! If clients insist on having the same mural, try to talk them into going for a smaller scale or pulling out the focal points of the original and enhancing them.

You are the artist, and the clients are relying heavily on you to tell them what the room dictates as far as composition, lighting requirements, and theme. Don't hesitate to tell them if you know the idea they're suggesting will have a poor outcome. If, after you've stated your misgivings, they insist on carrying out their vision anyway, put in writing your reasons for dissuading them and have them initial it. You might want to also stipulate the charges involved if you have to start over due to the dissatisfaction you're sure they will feel.

Bidding the Job

When bidding a mural, take several minutes to "live" with the room before tossing out ideas. Don't let the client hurry you with this process. Take a good look around. Where do the doors fall? Is it worth it to "wrap" the mural onto the wall where windows take up 98 percent of the area? What about that peaked ceiling on the west wall? Will your mural have to extend up to the ceiling at that point? Are there old radiators, soffits, built-ins, etc., that must be worked around or included in the mural's design?

The most important factor in deciding a mural's placement and theme is furniture placement. If the room is empty at the time of the interview, ask where the furnishings will be placed when the room is decorated. A large piece, such as a bed or sofa, will determine placement of the mural's elements; you don't want to spend hours painting detailed walls only to have a large piece of furniture blocking it.

Tell the clients that the room's furnishings are key to your layout of the mural. Ask if they anticipate moving the furniture around at a later date or changing the room entirely when JoBeth goes off to college. Do they plan on changing the fabric of the curtains or upholstery? This will affect the mural's color selection. Does the husband's moose-head trophy need to stay centered on your focal wall?

What color is the room's wood trim? If the wood is a dark cherry or mahogany, this can impact your mural and its "mood." Maple wood has a golden glow and would look lovely with fall aspens, where the darker wood might complement an oak tree. Painted white trim goes with everything and adds a crisp edge. Are there competing wood elements in the room? Is there an oak dresser with an ash-wood sleigh bed? If so, try not to bring in yet another wood hue in the mural to fight with the others.

You see? Living with a room for a moment and taking in all its features is very important. If you need a moment, tell the client this is an important part of determining the best ideas for the room. Ask for a few moments to concentrate. Then call them in and dazzle them with your plans to magically transform the room.

Here is where taking a moment to take in the room's special features pays off. That incredible idea you just came up with for having raccoons peering down from above the door wouldn't have occurred to you moments before, when you were concentrating solely on the main wall that will depict a forest scene. Offering to paint a portable mural of deer fawns to ride above the bed as a headboard has also magically appeared in your vision for the room and you extol it with enthusiasm.

Once you have your ideas in place and the client has interjected their thoughts and dreams for the room, *ask questions*! Get out your sketchpad and make a rough drawing of the room, including doors, windows, closets, etc. Now, get down to business.

With your drawing in hand, point to each wall, soffit, door, etc. and ask, "Are we doing anything with this wall (door, window blind, etc.)? Are we taking the paint up onto the ceiling?" If they say no, place a large "X" on that area of your sketch, showing it is not to be painted. Have them initial it. Make a very quick sketch showing the layout of the mural and any other elements you will be painting around the room.

One area often overlooked for murals is closet doors. They are easily replaced or painted over down the road when the mural has served its purpose. They make great castle doors for a child's room, or a Parisian café. For a recreation room, they might double as an English pub or Egyptian tomb. Think outside the canvas! The same goes for kitchen cabinets. Would an antiqued pear lightly rendered over a distressed European wash give the room a finished and unique look? Don't forget the bathroom; take that English garden you just wrapped the room in and toss some ivy crawling along the cabinet fronts.

Another area is window shades. Though they are not as prevalent as they once were, some homes and businesses still have them, and they are great spaces for murals: sunsets, birds, a view of ocean or mountain.

I was asked to paint fourteen wall murals in a beautiful Italian-style villa a few years ago. The dining room was two stories high with a balcony on one end that served as a place to put plants. I came up with the idea of turning the entire dining room into an Italian plaza with "rooms" overhead and people looking down on the festivities. I painted three scenes on canvas from a roll purchased at an art store. They measured 7' × 4', painted on pre-gessoed canvas. When they were completed, I adhered them to opposing walls with wallpaper vinyl adhesive, making sure all the air bubbles were out by using a squeegee with a light cloth over it to protect the painted surface. Then, to give them a realistic look, we added real shutters on each end of the "window"

which I had distressed to emulate an old Tuscan feel. We also added some left over trim at the bottom of the window to further the illusion. The shutters were only $10 a pair and it really made the illusion work as well as complement the trim used throughout the home.

They were so happy with the illusion that we added a large 8' × 8' section on the balcony where the plants were of a fake balcony scene with balusters, potted plants, and skyview. On the sides of the canvas I painted blowing curtains.

The next item of business was to paint the ceiling to look like a beautiful blue afternoon sky with subtle clouds and hues of an impending sunset. The total effect in the room now looked as if you were seated in an Italian plaza.

Now that you've gone over the sketch and ideas with the client, ask for a moment to estimate the cost. If you prefer to take the sketch back to your studio and work up the bid there, that's fine. I prefer to do it on the spot, while the client is excited and has the room's vision fresh in his mind. Take your time here! Don't rush or allow for a multitude of interruptions. Itemize each wall, headboard, closet door, ceiling, and light switch. Then go over it again! You may be in a hurry to give them the quote and get a deposit, but this will come back to haunt you later if you don't take your time now.

Once you are pleased with your thorough sweep of the room and have it all down, sit down with the client and go over each wall or feature. Tell them the reasons for each item on your breakdown and its cost. For instance, if you are doing a headboard, let them know you had to factor in the wood, primer, and sealer. If you are carting a piece of furniture to and from your studio, explain your travel costs. Perhaps a closet door or built-in will require some prep work, such as sanding, priming, etc., before you can begin; explain this. If you are adding elements to a mural to make it appear 3-D, such as adding real shutters, factor that into the price.

Beware of the clients who offer to do the sanding, priming, and other preliminary steps of a project to "help you out." While this can be handy if you don't like that part of the job, they can nickel and dime you for their part in it. *Put in writing the breakdown of costs for their part of the project and yours.* Most people do not realize the time involved in prep work.

Most artists who offer both murals and faux painting in their line of work bid murals by the day and bid faux by the square foot. I tend to bid both by the day. I average $400-$600 a day whether it is faux or murals, with some projects at $1000 a day. After you have rendered a few murals or finishes you will get a feel for how long it took you. I can eyeball a room now and know how long it will take me to do a particular finishing technique or mural, depending on the detail.

A frequent question you will hear is, "How much would you charge to do a child's room?"

I typically respond that it depends on how large the wall is, what texture the wall is and what subject I would be painting. "I can paint a Winnie-the-Pooh in 45 minutes, but something with more detail, like Spiderman, would take longer. I prefer to see the room and the area you want painted, brainstorm some ideas, and give you an estimate. The conference meeting is free." This type of approach seems to present a pretty clear picture of your bidding process and it works well for me to easily convey how the bidding is broken down.

One of the reasons I like the "daily breakdown" bid is that the estimate I give them is for the finished mural. Therefore, if I happen to finish it earlier than I planned, they will still owe me the agreed upon amount as they have the requested finished mural. If you are bidding it by the hour and you finish early, you are out some of the money you could have made by bidding it as simply a one-time project. There is the flip side in that you could go overtime and then the hourly rate would be to your benefit, but I don't like the stress of "being on the clock" and feeling as if they are monitoring my lunch breaks and watching to see if I am making good use of the time. I tend to create murals in a time efficient manner and it is one of the biggest compliments I get, but I just don't enjoy knowing someone is watching the clock. You can decide what works best for you.

Obviously, if you are using the eyeballing it and giving a flat rate for the job technique, you will need to give them an idea of how long you think it will take you. Again, with experience, you will know how long it will take. I generally add an extra day to allow for delays or *small* add-ons. Always allow several days between projects. Nothing will stress you out more than having project after project breathing down your neck when you are running behind. It also allows you to add more to a current project, which happens up quite often.

Listen carefully to any questions or concerns the clients may have. This is where I mention my free touch-up service and guarantee for their mural's durability. I go over what cleaning solvents are approved to prevent damage to the mural's surface. (I tell them no abrasives, such as Comet, which can destroy the surface. Simple soap and water is best. If it is more intrusive than that, a little 409 can be used but sparingly. Alcohol will fade the colors and remove some entirely.)

After all the questions have been answered and the total tallied, go over your schedule with them and select the appropriate date(s). Write down on the invoice the date(s) selected and the time you are to arrive and depart, if this is a stipulation; most businesses will require that you leave at closing time.

Ask for half down as a deposit to reserve the date and cover your material costs. Write their check number, or specify "cash," if cash is offered, next to the half-down amount on the invoice, and initial it. Have them initial it as well. This is now their receipt of the financial transaction.

If a detailed sketch is asked for, write that down, as well as the date you are to deliver it. List any samples of fabric, tile, photos, etc., the client may give you to take back to your studio. Always put these in a protective plastic bag and in a safe place at home. Some items they loan you are irreplaceable and carry great sentimental value.

You may be required to do some research before beginning the project, such as finding the right ocean view or street in Tuscany. If you feel this will take up a great deal of your time, you may want to add this to your bid. (I always do this gratis, as any excuse I have to go to a bookstore or library is fine with me. As always the Internet is a great resource tool. I use Google's image feature to find dozens of photos for elements I need in a mural.) If they are doing the legwork, set a date to get back together to go over ideas.

The Latest Mural Techniques

While mural techniques may not have exploded to the point that the faux painting industry has, there are some fun ways to render exquisite murals being developed all over. We will break them down in chapter 10 and discuss their different elements and bidding strategies. Here are just a few:

- **Frescoes** utilize crackling mediums and textures to create Old World finishes resembling the aged walls of European buildings, palaces, cottages, and farmhouses. These finishes are also used on furnishings, creative décor, and even old book covers.
- **Caulking** designs can be drawn onto a wall with caulking compound such as tub and tile caulk and, when dry, can be painted in any color to give your walls a 3-D look.
- **Dimensional stenciling** can be done on wall murals by using large die-cut stencils and an embossing method using mediums such as dimensional craft paints and Venetian plaster.
- **Stamping** can be utilized in simple wall murals where elementary elements are needed such as small flowers, butterflies, etc. These work well in a children's mural. You can find a plethora of stamp pads, as well as lettering styles, at hobby stores.
- **Gilding** can be incorporated into a mural for a very dramatic effect, such as copper gilding on a Tuscan roof or the dome of a building. Anything that would be gold, bronze, or copper in real life can be rendered in leafing on a wall. This would require a special sealant to protect the delicate finish.
- **Metallic paints** can create a similar effect to that of gilding for much less cost and are more durable. When lighting is directed onto them, they can appear as if they are on fire.
- **Plasters** in varying mediums can be used as a build-up process to make your walls come to life. I have even used vinyl wall spackle to create texture and build out an element of a painting. Check your home center stores and ask about their plasters and purposes.
- **Fluorescent paints** used with a black light can create fun murals that glow in the dark.
  You can use Prismatic Paints that come in oil and water-based mediums. You can even create these murals to work with 3-D glasses! Talk about a kid's paradise!
- **Foils** are now being introduced into murals with striking results. Hologram foil is especially effective in creating that metallic, dimensional look. These are called metallic foils and can be found online or in specialty interior design facilities.

- **Cement** has left the driveway and found its way onto walls. Artists are using it to create three-dimensional walls of stone, trees, and much, much more. The typical medium used is called Flex-C-Ment and is manufactured by Yoder and Son. When applied over a concrete primer it can be sculpted, stamped and sprayed, hand brushed, and detailed with paint, to create some amazing effects that will have your clients wondering if it is real or not.
- **Crackle** mediums can be used to antique a mural giving it warmth and dimension.
- **Airbrushing** has always been a popular method with muralists wanting to make realistic skies, seascapes, and anything to appear almost 3-D. You will require special equipment for this art form and hours of practice with frisket and other masking mediums.

There are as many techniques out there as there are imaginative minds! I have seen murals created with mosaic tiles, jewelry, plant parts, fabric pieces, and even car parts. You are only as limited as your imagination! Gary Lord has a wonderful book out called *Mural Painting: Secrets for Success* by North Light Books. It is filled with wonderful mural ideas and advice.

Furniture, Screens, and Much More

This area can cover myriad ideas, mediums, and treatments. I have painted murals on furniture, antique horse-drawn sleighs, tire covers, boats, RVs, garage doors, canisters, cabinets, dresser faces, cribs, headboards, closets, tools, plaques, barnwood—you name it.

When bidding murals for furniture, keep in mind that the mural is only part of it. You must factor in sanding the area if it had varnish on it at one time, which is probably the case. You can't paint over varnish—the acrylics will resist it and it will not be durable. Sanding it will bring up a tooth enabling you to paint. You will probably want a sealant over it when finished. You may have to use a varnish remover or other solvent to get down to the area needed. You need to consider your time for using a tack cloth to remove sanding residue, removing and replacing hardware, possibly painting inside crevices and drawers, and hauling materials in and out.

If you are doing a distressed look, you may be using waxes and metallics. Plan every step in your head and write them down, estimating the time it will take for each one.

Room screens or dividers have made a comeback with Oriental designs still leading the way. I have been asked to paint wildlife, Hollywood Deco, fairytales, topiaries, faux finishes, and antique cars. Golf motifs are also popular, along with aquatic, Italian, or anything with an Old World influence.

When bidding screens, take into consideration all your time in buying the wood panels (found at home centers in the lumber section), having them cut down to size or cutting them yourself, sanding, priming, basecoating, and installing hardware. Then add in your mural work!

I like using a good quality board such as MDF. Plywood can have a graining you don't want in your design. There are factory-sanded boards that work well. Check to make sure there are no imperfections on either side, such as knotholes or chips. Look down the length of the board to check for warping or distortions. I prefer a ½" to 1" depth depending on the size. If I am doing a smaller screen, such as one used for a fireplace screen, I use ½". For taller panels that range from 4' to 8', I like a thicker board so that it retains its shape and doesn't fall over.

When bidding other objects brought to you for mural painting, just keep in mind any time needed to prepare a quality surface. Walk the client through the prep stages so that they understand where costs for time and materials come in. Many people only think of the mural and not what goes into preparing something to be painted. If a sealant is needed, add that in as well. If you are dealing with a family heirloom or an expensive item, have your clients sign a waiver relieving you of blame if the painting technique yellows or somehow distorts the original surface. Be very careful with items that cannot be replaced or hold great sentimental value. If possible, experiment on a similar surface to test for any side effects that could occur from your paint mediums.

A Word about Ceilings

Ceilings are tiring. Period. End of sentence. You may be in great physical shape, but your neck muscles are going to be tired after rendering a ceiling. A ceiling mural will take longer than you planned, so bid accordingly. You may have to work around obstacles such as built-ins, furniture that has been merely pushed to one side instead of removed from the room. Curtain rods, crown molding, and wall brackets can all be a source of irritation when you're trying to jockey for position on a ceiling painting.

Draping a room is imperative when you're painting ceilings. One drop on a cherished bedspread could signal your doom. Cover everything! Use lightweight plastic drop cloths to cover dresser tops, computers, etc. Tape plastic sheeting over drapery tops and cornices. Have floors completely covered.

When moving ladders or scaffolding around, move slowly and watch for baseboards and furniture. If you are bringing scaffolding or large equipment in through the house, have a trail of tarps leading from the door to the area you are working in to walk upon. Have a partner help with heavy equipment to avoid scratching floors or walls.

Take stretch breaks when painting ceilings, and rotate your neck and shoulders. Allow extra time and break the mural down into doable sections for each day's work.

> **TIP:** Don't paint directly overhead; this leads to drips falling into your eyes and face. Paint slightly to the left or right of your head and, if rolling on paint, roll ahead of yourself or behind.

Dealing with Children's Rooms

My main rule for painting murals in children's rooms is to include the child in the decision-making process. Listen to their likes and dislikes. This can sometimes be a little difficult if the parents have their own view of the room and it differs from the child's. In my experience parents tend to want the fantasies they had as children. Mother may want the fairytale castle room with a knight flourishing a flag as he rides over a green hill toward a castle painted in cotton-candy pink. The little girl may want dragonflies and skateboards. If a compromise can't be reached, you may have to tactfully withdraw and ask them to call you when they've worked it out.

This dispute factor can also happen between a father and mother who have two different visions for Ralph or Cecilia's room. Recently, I did a little boy's room in a celestial motif, because his favorite book his mother read to him each night had a mother-moon-and-little-star theme. We painted the book's cover design on the ceiling in a field of blue and stars and fauxed the walls in denim. The father, however, wanted a baseball theme, as his son loved sports equally. The compromise was that the baseball theme would be carried out in the bedspread and throw pillows and I would come back at a later date and add bats and balls around the walls. Go into a child's room with an open mind to color scheme. Offer something other than the expected blue for the boy and pink for the girl. Bend the gender rules a little and come up with something innovative. Primary colors are also overworked in children's rooms. Use the primary color wheel if you wish, but use cranberry instead of bright red or periwinkle instead of navy blue. Peach colors and soft sage greens are beautiful and don't tire the eye the way intense hues can. Remember to inform the client of how color can open up or close in a room. Most children's rooms tend to be on the small side, and you want to "push the walls out." Powder blues and pale greens will visually move the walls out and so are good choices here. The bright warm colors, such as reds, oranges, and yellow, will advance the walls and make the room feel smaller.

The fantasy world of children and teenagers opens the doors to the creative genius of a good artist. Have fun and offer something unique. Study the room and try to get a feel for the child's likes and collections. If the bedspread sports dolphins, perhaps an aquatic theme would be fun and would keep the feeling of continuity flowing.

Cowboy themes are making a comeback, at least here in Colorado, and lariats are again hanging from headboards and ponies adorning walls. I recently bid a young man's room where they wanted an Old West town painted on the focal wall (the main wall you see as you enter a room). I suggested adding a few fun elements around the rest of the room. We came up with a giant cactus cut out of MDF board, with a stand. This would double as a place to hang cowboy hats and pajamas. I then recommended cutting cowboy boots out of plywood and painting them on both sides. These would become wall brackets to hold shelves for souvenirs and toys. The final touch was to take the child's photograph, scan it, and turn it into a "Wanted" poster for the wall . . . complete with a reward in case of his capture!

Recently I bid a young girl's room that was based on the Disney Princesses. Around the room were a few of the vinyl decals they had purchased of Cinderella and Sleeping Beauty, but the room lacked a cohesive mural feel. I painted landscape to go with the vinyl figures and then noticed that the child's bed was simply on a frame without a headboard. I mentioned that I could create a fairytale castle from plywood that would double as a headboard. The headboard turned out to be 7' high. It was cut out from wood and included a section with a clock tower. The area for the clock was cut out from the board leaving a round 12" hole exposed. I then placed a pale yellow piece of Plexiglas (which I bought as a remnant from a sign company) behind the hole and bought clock hands and vinyl clock face numerals from a hobby store. A small hole was drilled into the center of the Plexiglas and the hands attached. I glued the numerals around the clock. Behind the Plexiglas, on the back of the headboard, I attached a small nightlight that you can buy in any home center, with a switch halfway down the cord to allow the child to turn it off and on easily. Now my clock face lit up at night and doubled as a built-in nightlight. I also cut out the area where the drawbridge would go and placed a small curtain rod behind it, attaching it to the back of the castle. I sewed a lavender satin curtain with a pocket to slide over the rod. The curtains parted in the middle. The drawbridge area was now a puppet theatre!

There is no better place to come alive with your talent than this arena. If your client is having a hard time coming up with ideas, show her some books of children's room themes. If she gets excited about a certain theme, improve upon it and add your own special signature.

You will be asked to render murals from the latest children's movies, whether in private homes or businesses. This can be a challenge if the movie has been advertised far in advance and the books about the film have not yet hit the bookstores for you to use as references. You can try Googling the movie to see if some photos pop up there. As I was finishing this book, *How to Train Your Dragon* had just hit the theatres and the kids were going wild over it. I was asked to paint it in a pediatric dental office. It was a huge hit.

I like to add 3-D touches when possible to throw in a dash of realism and whimsy. Try suspending magic wands from the ceiling using monofilament line if you are painting a room based on wizards, magic, fairies, etc. They should be out of reach of the child. You can make wands from simple wood dowels purchased at an art store, paint 3/4 of it black and the final 1/4 in silver. Drill a small hold in the end of the silver portion and glue in sparkling foils purchased from a party store. The wands will twirl in the room's air current, giving the illusion that magic is always going on.

Commercial sites ask for children's themes as well. Since you generally have a larger area to work with than in a residential setting, you can have a lot of fun! I created a wonderful area of magic, enchanted forests, wizards, magicians, wood elves, and dragons in a recent dental clinic. Let your imagination go wild!

Some parents worry about paint fumes in their child's room, especially an infant's. Assure them the acrylics have minimal, if any, odor, and dry in ten minutes. Lead was eliminated from paints years ago and is no longer a factor in determining a wall's finish.

Nap times may have to be worked around with small children. Most parents will have the child sleep somewhere else to accommodate you, but occasionally you may run into one who insists the child's routine be maintained. Be nice but firm in letting them know your own routine and that it may incur an additional charge if you have to keep starting and stopping your work.

Commercial Sites

There are a few guidelines to keep in mind when painting murals for businesses:

1. Commercial clients will be much more stringent in their time frames for your work hours. You may be told you cannot paint during operating hours and will have to come back in the evening or on weekends. You will have to decide if the job is worth it to you or if you will charge more for the inconvenience.
2. You will be dealing with several more personalities when working on commercial sites, as you will be working around staff, employees, customers, and sometimes construction workers. Put on your best game face and practice patience, patience, patience.
3. If painting around an office or desk area, you may have to plan certain sections of the mural to be painted during the employee's break or lunch hour. Luckily, the paint dries fast, and you can move their desk back quickly or hang up the picture Aunt Effie painted of their favorite pet poodle.
4. When on commercial sites, you will have a lot of people watching you paint. If this makes you nervous or slows you down, you may want to skip business murals. I enjoy the interaction with people,

especially little kids when painting preschools. If the interruptions become too much and they involve the businesses' employees, you may have to speak to someone about it.

5. If painting a hallway or busy traffic area, seal it off temporarily, and finish the painting as quickly as possible. Paint stores sell "wet paint" ribbons that can be stretched around a work area. Arrange with the owner ahead of time for the area needing to be cordoned off. Assure them acrylic paint dries in ten to fifteen minutes and business can continue as usual without fear of damaging the walls or getting paint on customers' clothes.

6. Try to compartmentalize your work areas, so your things are not scattered all over. Break down the job into rooms or walls and keep everything in a neat, organized work area. Keep tarps taped down, so customers cannot trip over bunched edges. If you are working under a store's roof, you are responsible for their customers' safety when it comes to your equipment and supplies.

7. Courtesy is your hallmark when you're working around businesses—courtesy to their staff and especially to their customers. If you have to get down off a ladder a hundred times to allow the entrance door to be opened and closed, do it with a smile.

8. Have plenty of business cards with you to hand out. You will be asked by the staff and customers if they like your work. Commercial sites are a great way to advertise your work . . . and your personality.

9. Take special care to leave public bathrooms clean and paint-free. Wipe up water spills on the floor and always wipe out the sink and faucets with a dry paper towel.

10. Ask where to park your vehicle and through which door to bring in your things. The owner may not want you coming and going through the main entrance.

Work closely with the owner and involve him in the decision-making process. Try to get with the client before his busy day kicks in. If questions should arise during business hours, ask a secretary or someone else to ask if he has a minute to consult with you. Keep the interruptions to a minimum.

Make sure you have all your supplies with you to avoid borrowing pencils, tape, etc. Secretaries and staff are busy, too, and have their own work to do. Take their lead as to whether they want to chitchat or prefer you to remain invisible.

At the end of the day, stack your things in the area set aside for you or load them into your vehicle. Double-check to see if you've left anything out. Throw away all food wrappers, cans, bottles, etc., and restore furniture you've moved back to its original position.

If you are the last to leave, ask ahead of time if you are to turn out all the lights and lock the doors. Most businesses leave a major light on to discourage theft, and the door may need to be left open for janitorial services. Find out and follow the rules to the letter.

A few final words about commercial sites: never go through drawers, cabinets, or closets for any reason. You don't want to be accused of misplacing an important memo, or, worse, stealing something. Don't use the phone without asking, as you can mess up their phone system by pressing the wrong button. And *never* unplug anything without asking!

Setting Up Your Paint Kit

With murals, I sometimes feel as if I'm packing my entire studio. The night before a project, I try to simplify things by organizing my paint kit from the last job and tossing out any used tubes of paint. I have a large plastic craft tote from an arts-and-craft store and several clear plastic receptacles stacked inside, holding tubes of paint. The paints are divided into color groups, e.g., browns, yellows, blues, etc. This way I can lift out each tray as needed and put it back when I move on to another color group. It also shows me at a glance if I'm running low on a certain color. When using my favorite cart on wheels, I transfer the colors I need for the mural at that time into the middle drawer, but always keep a ready supply of extra paint in the tote, especially white and black.

Some artists prefer to mix their own colors, using only a handful of large acrylic tubes or pigments. I must confess I enjoy having all the premixed colors of acrylics in the handy squirt bottles. If I need a soft shade of lavender, it's right there, ready with its handy flip-top lid. Bulk up on white and black acrylics in the large economy sizes. If the mural you're doing that day requires a large amount of sky or hillside, take along large containers of blue and green and then add colors to customize its outcome.

I use paint trays for my palette as I'm dealing with large surfaces: mainly walls. Take along several compartmentalized plastic plates or sturdy paper plates for small amounts of paint. To outline cartoon characters, I take along plastic cups to hold the black or dark-brown paint. This allows me to move along quickly without stooping over a tray or plate. I've seen many artists using large plastic cups taped together into a portable palette, but the color selection is too limiting for me. I prefer to mix the colors in a large tray.

Of course, you will need your tarps, masking tape, and sharpened pencils. Home center stores such as Lowe's and Home Depot carry carpenter's pencils that are wonderful! They are hard red plastic holders with refillable lead that comes out as needed. They use extra hard lead so there is less smearing and you use less lead. When the point wears down, you simply slip the head holder down and more lead appears. Most come with extra lead cartridges. I have now completed four large medical clinics and have yet to use up one cartridge. I realize some artists prefer drawing with chalk or pastels, but I still like using a pencil. I find chalk can accidentally be removed by your arm or clothing while painting or drawing other elements. Every artist has his or her own favorite technique. *Tip: Some dollar stores sell giant pink erasers with a broad face that are wonderful for large projects such as murals. They are roughly 4" to 5" long. I have used mine on four major projects and have barely dented it.*

Extra paper towels are always handy. Have a few marine sponges in different sizes available for adding texture to treetops, stone walls, grassy knolls, etc. Keep an assortment of foam brushes with you as well. These are wonderful for smooth transference of paints and blending.

A few years ago, my son gave me a wonderful carrying kit for all my artist's brushes. It converts to a standing position so that I can select the brush I need without hassle. Keep your brushes stored in some kind of carrying case where their bristles won't be compromised.

A hand cleaner and brush cleaner are good to have along. Paint left to dry in the brush's ferrule will ruin it. Save your ruined brushes with the splayed hairs for dabbing on textured bark and rock. An old toothbrush is great for "spatter," to create life-like rocks and star clusters.

Rulers, yardsticks, and levels should be included in your kit. Take along various sizes, as sometimes you may be penciling a stone block wall and you'll be stuck in a tight space where a full yardstick won't fit. Again, there are fancy laser levels and measuring devices out there as well. These can cover large areas that you would normally "snap" off with a plumb line and free you from needing another person or anchoring one end of the plumb line with a thumbtack.

If you're rendering stencils, have along your stencil adhesive spray, acetate stencils, stencil brushes, and paints. Here again, a level or measuring device comes in handy. An X-ACTO blade is also good to have.

Pack a screwdriver with a Phillips and flathead bit to remove switch plates, unless you're painting over them. If you have quarts or gallons of paint for this job, throw in your paint key or can opener. A flathead screwdriver can also be used here.

Make sure you have your references for your mural, such as photos, books, or illustrations. Wrap them in plastic wrap to keep paint from ruining their surfaces. Libraries are especially particular about their books being returned with added adornment.

Take along a small tub of spackle for unexpected holes in the wall. Clients may remove pictures or shelving units before you come, and you are suddenly looking at a series of holes; these work well with gangster murals but little else.

You can place a can of soda and some snacks in your paint kit along with a cell phone. I place my car keys in my kit while I'm painting, so I always know where they are. A notepad for notes to yourself or the client is a good idea as well.

Finally, pack a pencil sharpener, whether manual or electric. Always have extra pencils and erasers ready.

Your kit is packed, and you're ready to go. Now load a small stepstool or folding chair in the car for you to sit on while painting the midsection of the wall. A six-to-eight-foot stepladder will be necessary for most of the upper wall. If you have to go higher than that, decide on the proper equipment. You can rent scaffolding by the half-day, day, or week. Be sure to include your rental fees in the bid.

Pack your water bucket, tarps, rags, empty trash bags for used paper towels and ruined foam brushes, CD player, bottled water, and business cards. If there is no source of running water where you'll be painting, load a five-gallon bucket half-full of hot water. (If you load a full bucket, your car's interior will resemble an aquarium by the time you reach the job site.)

NOTE TO SELF: *Remember to take the client's address and phone number, in case you get lost.*

Supplies

The area of supplies and which ones serve the muralist better is open to interpretation. You can have a room full of muralists and see a dozen different paint setups. When I first started out, I had all manner of talented people coming up to me on commercial sites telling me I was using the wrong brush or offering suggestions for a more expedient way to do things. At first, I felt embarrassed and thought I must look amateurish.

As the years went by, I adopted the brushes and techniques that worked for *me*. I developed a consistent speed and style, and to change my way of doing things now would feel unfamiliar and probably impede my work. I'm all for the new revolutions in technology, and I love trying new tools if they seem superior to what I have, but my basic supply setup hasn't changed much in the past ten years.

In chapter 12 you will find a section entitled "Master List of Materials, Supplies, and Equipment." Here you will find an extensive list of supplies to use for both murals and faux painting. For now, let me mention some of the most important parts of your art kit.

Your first goal will be to go out and buy some *good* brushes. I realize paying anywhere from $12 to $45 for a brush can cause a queasy feeling in your stomach. They will pay for themselves in the long run. The inferior brushes will lose hairs all over your mural and fall apart faster than you can say "Bob Ross." Buy brushes made especially for your medium. I use only acrylics, so I buy the synthetic brushes stipulated for acrylic use. Some animal-hair brushes are also used with acrylic, so read the labels carefully. Your brushes will fall into these categories:

- Round brushes, used mainly for detailing
- Flat brushes, ideal for blending and graduating color, as in skies, and for stippling foliage effects

- Fan brushes, used for flowers, tree tops, and some water effects
- Filberts, round sturdy brushes which take a lot of abuse, great for a number of special effects
- Liner brushes and scroll brushes, used for lettering and fine detail, as in animal hair and outline
- Decorator's brushes, in one-, two-, three- and four-inch widths, used for covering large areas of walls and priming wall surfaces before painting

You will also need rollers and paint pads for painting large areas and ceilings. Buy a short-pile roller, as you'll create a more even surface than with the long-pile types. I use the paint pads to triple-load paint and fill in quick, realistic ocean backgrounds and hillsides.

Marine sponges in all shapes and types (wool, elephant ear, natural) come in handy to render fast treetops, clouds, grass, bushes, and mist.

If you need to transfer a pattern or logo to your mural surface, take along graphite transfer paper found at art stores and some craft stores.

A calculator, string (to determine perspective lines), thumbtacks (to hold the string), and sandpaper finish out the list of supplies used most often in creating murals.

Some artists use airbrushes and that requires a whole new set of supplies, including a generator. Again, this area is a very personal one, and you should take your time selecting your tools; they'll be with you a long time and will make all the difference in the quality of your work.

Plagiarism

Very often you will be asked to copy another artist's work onto a wall or decorative surface. This happens frequently in children's rooms, where the child has a favorite cartoon or film character they want reproduced on their wall. I'm sure Thomas Kincade has been ripped off for wall murals more times than he can count. Disney would probably garner the highest honors in this category.

This is an area where I can't counsel you. It is obvious from the numbers of Disney-related themes in daycares, preschools, and homes that the copyright law has been bent frequently in the mural business. Many believe that if you are painting a private home or business, you are not stepping on any legal toes. Short of turning out rip-off designs on the mass market, artists take quite a few liberties here.

If you are hoping to paint some major project with copyrighted work, get permission first! Don't end up with legal fees and fines because you thought you would not get caught.

Many years ago, an article appeared in a local paper about Disney's concern over the amount of plagiarism going on with its products. Since it emphasized products, I wondered if painting private homes with wall murals fell under that umbrella. Be careful when using copyrighted material, if you use it at all.

When To Say No

When you first start out in this business, it is so easy to say yes to every request. You are so grateful for any work or recognition that comes your way. You will underbid a job just to land it, swearing that the next time you will get paid what you are worth. This is common. But there will be times when walking away from a demanding client or an unworkable situation is required. No amount of money is worth having someone spitefully take advantage of a new artist. There are personalities out there that will take all they can get and will want to pay minimally for it. There are also times when the working conditions are so poor, that it would be unfair to ask anyone to work under such restrictive situations.

I have been in the middle of a few projects before realizing there would never be a way to please a particular client. I became a slave instead of an artisan. One woman cornered me every day I was painting to waste hours of my time showing me albums of her children's vacations, costumes she had made for them, and generally talking my ear off. At first I was gracious and understood her need to brag about her children. But as I watched my deadline come and go and my stress level rose, I could no longer handle it. I had other work breathing down my neck and no amount of reasoning with her was working. I had tactfully told her that I was getting behind, and while I appreciated her commitment to her children, if she wanted the mural finished in the quality way we had discussed and for the price we had agreed upon, she would have to leave me alone to do my work. It didn't even make a dent! The next day she actually spread a blanket on the floor behind me, complete with a picnic lunch and talked non-stop for five hours, at times thrusting photos of her children in front of my face as I painted.

We had agreed on four walls to wrap the room in fairytale castles, golden coaches, princesses, and meadows. I was only a quarter of the way through when the deadline was one day away. I finished the one wall and told her I could not complete the room as I was now due on other projects. She was furious. I pointed out how many times I had asked her to let me get my work done without interruption, but she couldn't understand it. She refused to pay for the entire project even though it had taken me the time it would have to do all four walls. I had a decision to make. I settled for charging her only for the wall completed and made up my mind that I would never be put in that position again. If a client started down that road, I would stop immediately, make my working needs known and if they could not comply, I would quit then and there before wasting my time.

Often you will get a "gut feeling" about someone. Trust that instinct and walk away. If you are allergic to pet hair or cigarette smoke, don't put yourself through it. There are other jobs. Sometimes you will get (especially early on) the people who offer to "help" you out. You paint a mural for them for free and they will advertise your business and hand out your cards. I will admit to doing this in a restaurant when I was starting out to get more business. This is your call. Sometimes it is advantageous, sometimes not so much. It is all part of the growing process. Use your gut feeling for whether you think there is real business potential.

You will also be approached with the good old barter system. They will offer you products or services in exchange for your artwork. Sometimes this works out well. If you are being offered products, such as retail items, they should trade you out at cost, not the retail price. You are not marking up your supplies. They may argue that you are taking items that someone else would have paid full price for and therefore are costing them money. You can volley back with the fact you are not charging them tax on your supplies or simply mark your price up accordingly. Make sure you are getting equal value for your time and materials. This can be a slippery slope. Get everything in writing!

The world of murals is full of potential. The avenues for success in this field are varied and wide reaching. It can snowball quickly, and suddenly you find yourself in Georgia painting walls for the gentlemen who saw your work in Kentucky. Travel plans and travel expenses will all have to be figured in when you reach this stage.

I would like to end this section by stating something that may seem obvious, but that I feel is worth reiterating. When you accept payment for your artwork, you have now crossed the line from a hobbyist to a professional. You are taking on an entirely new mantle of responsibility. You have no way of knowing how much a client may have wrestled with the decision to let go of that $600 they are offering to pay you. I have found out later that people have foregone vacations, household furnishings, and even some courses they were going to take to further their own careers in order to have a mural done for their child, or somewhere else in their home or business. This has never ceased to remind me of my responsibility to turn out the most professional work I can muster. Even homes that look affluent often carry hefty mortgages or the owners are struggling with a falling stock market or changes in their business cash flow. Treat everyone the same and never lose your gratitude for making a living that most of the world considers a dream job. It took the recession that started hitting hard in the fall of 2008 to remind me how good I had it. The mural work came to a sudden halt. Murals were a luxury, not a necessity, and I suddenly found myself feeling as if I had just started out, rather than having thirty-two years of experience under my belt. I was trying every unique form of advertising I could find to drum up business and even went back to blanketing neighborhoods with flyers. Let me tell you, that is one humbling wake-up call. Now I treasure every job I have and I have a renewed love of this career that, admittedly, I had started to take for granted and even hit a few burn-out months along the way. You are truly blessed to be able to make a living by using a talent! Please never take it for granted! Just remember those golden rules in this business: Exceptional service, perseverance, competitive prices, and excellent quality. And remember, "Quality is long remembered after price is forgotten."

What a thrill!

10

TODAY'S TECHNIQUES, SUPPLIES, TOOLS, AND BIDDING STRATEGIES

The following information is meant to be helpful for those of you just starting out and trying to decipher the myriad tools, techniques, and bidding requirements of the world of faux and murals. I have attempted to put today's techniques into categories that tend to utilize the same equipment, glazes, and time requirements so that you will have a better feel of how to bid each job based on the number of glazes for that project, specialty additives such as plaster, cement or other elements, wall conditions, etc. Bidding a job when you are just starting out is formidable and it is my hope that this will give you a little more confidence to bid the job for the time it will take you and not underbid it out of fear of the technique or not enough confidence in your skills. This will become second nature to you as you do more and more jobs.

Keep in mind that some paint techniques require a great deal of time, such as Venetian plaster, collage, fossil rock, and some metallics. They also change the wall texture and cannot be simply painted over in the future when the client wants a new look. You must tell your customer when you bid the job that these motifs will have to be sanded down and they might even have to put in new plasterboard. Many other techniques today can be painted over without drastic sanding or using specialty primers.

Types of Paint

Most of today's faux finishing techniques are rendered in water-based paints, also called latex. These paints dry faster, are safer for the environment, and don't require strong solvents for clean-up. Some faux painters like to render elegant finishes in oil-based paints, also known as alkyds, which are much slower to dry and require solvents such as mineral spirits or turpentine.

Glazes are translucent films painted over a base-coated wall or surface to create visual effects and textures. Various tools are used with glazes to create a myriad of effects from marbling to fresco, parchment to frottage. Glazes are made by combining water, pigmented paint, and a glazing medium, which acts as a binder. These glazing mediums not only create the translucent look but also extend the drying time of water-based paints allowing the artist to manipulate them into the desired look. Glazing mediums have instructions on the can describing dilution and mixture requirements.

Primers and Sealers are very important when rendering today's finishes. These help cover flaws and provide a good base for the paint to adhere to. Primers are available for both water-based and oil-based paints. The more porous the surface, the more a sealant or primer is needed. Surfaces in good condition that are not porous do not always need this preliminary step.

Flat Latex Primer is used for sealing unfinished drywall or previously painted surfaces. Due to the fast drying time of this primer you can begin your faux finish or mural the same day.

Deep Color Primer is helpful when your finish will involve deep, dark colors. It can be tinted to match your color and give you a head start on using intense pigments. It can save you from having to do multiple coats of your painting medium.

Latex Enamel Primer is used primarily for sealing raw wood, closing the pores and providing a smooth top finish with which to work. Cedar, redwood, or plywood contains water-soluble dyes which will bleed through primer, so these are not good woods for this particular product.

Stain-Killing Primer such as Kilz can be used on walls with stains such as ink, grease, crayon, or heavy pigments that could bleed through your topcoat. They can also be used to seal knotholes in wood and are great for woods with water-soluble dyes such as cedar, redwood, and plywood.

Metal and Masonry Primer is used for metal, brick, or cement block surfaces, both for exterior and interior use. These come in various solutions, for areas that are rust-free and for those where rusting has begun. They inhibit rusting when applied and give you a surface that will allow the top coat to adhere evenly to the metal.

(**TIP**: If you want to remove rust from a project before applying primers and paints, try Naval Jelly. Ask your area home center if they stock it or try a reputable paint dealer or car-detailing establishment.)

Drying Times for Paints	
Water-Based	Oil-Based
Primers: 1-4 hours	Primers: 4-10 hours; do not recoat for 24 hrs.
Paints: 1-4 hours	Paints: 6-10 hours; do not recoat for 24 hrs.
Stains: 1-4 hours	Stains: 6-10 hours; do not recoat for 24 hrs.

To determine your time needed for various techniques, consider the following information for prep work needed for different surfaces.

Surface Preparation Guidelines		
Surface	Preparation	Primer
Unfinished Drywall	1. Sand surface 2. Wipe with tack cloth 3. Apply Primer	Flat latex primer
Painted Drywall	1. Clean surface to remove dirt 2. Rinse with clear water, let dry 3. Apply primer if dramatic color change.	Flat latex primer only if painting over spots or strong colors
Unpainted Plaster	1. Sand surface 2. Dust w/hand broom, vacuum	Polyvinyl acrylic primer
Painted Plaster	1. Clean surface of dirt & grease 2. Rinse w/clear water, let dry 3. Repair any cracks or holes 4. Sand surface to degloss/smooth	Polyvinyl acrylic primer only if painting over spots or dark colors

Surface Preparation Guidelines		
Unfinished Wood	1. Sand surface smooth 2. Wipe with tack cloth 3. Apply primer	Latex enamel undercoat
Painted Wood	1. Clean surface, remove dirt 2. Rinse with clear water, let dry 3. Sand surface lightly 4. Wipe with tack cloth 5. Apply primer	Latex enamel undercoat only on bare wood areas
Unfinished Metal	1. Remove rust, grease, etc. 2. Sand off any ragged edges 3. Apply primer	Metal primer, latex
Finished Metal	1. Use Naval Jelly to remove rust 2. Sand if necessary to remove old paint, stains or imperfections 3. Apply primer	Metal primer, latex
Concrete	1. If new concrete, allow a month to cure, some as much as 45-50 days to dry. Talk w/contractor. 2. Older concrete, remove stains, grease, rust, mold, etc. w/power washers, or brush and scrub w/ water and detergents. Do NOT use muriatic acid or other acidic solutions. 3. If staining a smooth surface such as a basement or garage floor, sand surface with 60-80 grit sandpaper. Patch chipped areas w/patching material made with cement.	Masonry primer

Providing a Quality Surface

Make sure your wall surfaces are clean and free of grease (a problem in a kitchen), dirt, crayon, lipstick, or sticky residue left from removing wallpaper. You can ask the client to have this taken of or charge them for your time and supplies to do so. If cracks are visible, they must be filled, sanded, and basecoated with the same paint sheen and color already existing on the wall. If pictures are removed and the client does not want the nails to remain, remove the nails and patch the holes with vinyl spackle, sand, and basecoat. Some molly bolts or plastic screw heads showing can be lightly hammered into the wall, then covered with spackle, sanded, and base painted.

Patch any holes in the drywall. This can be time-intensive. A rectangular hole must be cut using a drywall saw. A backer strip must then be cut from drywall or wood and hot-glued to the back of the opening. Cut a rectangular drywall patch slightly smaller than the opening, and secure it in place to the backing strips using hot glue.

At this point you will apply self-adhesive drywall tape over the cracks, then spackle. After drying, sand the area and apply PVA (polyvinyl acrylic) primer.

There are also self-adhering fiberglass and metal repair patches that simply go over the rectangular hole you have cut, and are then coated with spackle, sanded and primer applied.

Other prep work will include taping off doorways, windows, covering hanging light fixtures (if painting a ceiling), and removing furniture from the room or placing it in the center of the area and covering it with drop cloths. Remove items like window valances, draperies, and window treatment hardware such as rods and brackets. Tape off fireplaces, mantels, built-ins, countertops, and cabinet edges. Caulk that runs along backsplashes will resist tape. You may think you have it taped it down but odds are your faux glaze will puddle beneath it. I typically use a paint shield for these areas and wipe them after each paint application as I move along. Caulking in other areas, such as around doors, tub surrounds, etc., will also repel paint. You may have to go back with a liner brush and work paint into the caulk in a slightly thicker medium which will mean tinting down your paint color a little to allow for the reduced glaze and water.

If you are painting a ceiling, you may need to drape the walls with plastic, taped to the top of each wall to prevent paint from splattering down the surface. Make sure the entire floor is covered in tarps and all furniture, mantel tops and built-ins are covered and protected.

Today's Painting Techniques and Their Stages

Here we will try to subdivide the painting techniques into categories based on similar set-up time, tools, and time to render them. Covering this in a precise and scientific way is impossible, because each artist will incorporate his or her own style, speed, and embellishments. But this will give you a general rule of thumb with which to confidently bid the project based on materials, prep, and execution.

One-Stage Faux Painting Techniques

1. **Color Wash.** Satin latex paint, glazing medium, marine sponge or 4" to 6" paintbrush. If you are basecoating the wall in a color first to complement your color wash, then this is a two-part project. If not, you will be covering the walls in a one-step glaze. Bid based on time to go around the room once. I can cover an 12' × 8' wall in one hour using a one-step process.

2. **Sponging On or Off.** Satin latex paint, glazing medium, marine sponge. Again, if you are basecoating a color first, this becomes a two-part process. If not, you will be applying glaze to the wall with a sponge and manipulating it to resemble effects like Old World glazes. Sponging off is a two-part process in that it requires a glaze to be applied to the wall and then immediately sponged off, leaving only portions of the glaze behind. It is a technique. You can generally render these effects in a short period of time—one to two hours per 12' × 8' wall section.

3. **Ragging On or Off.** Satin latex paint, glazing mediums, clean cotton, lint-free cloths in 2'-square sections. Similar to sponging above, only using rags.

4. **Double Rolling.** Satin latex paint in two colors, glazing medium, double roller with divided paint tray. This technique requires a complementary background so a basecoat will probably be necessary before you begin rolling the area in your two paint colors poured side by side in a paint tray. You will be blending the two paint colors as you go with the double paint roller. A small, foam edging tool will be needed for corners and edges where the rollers can't fit tightly. Once the base coat is on, this is a very fast technique. Usually a 12' × 8' wall section can be rendered in an hour or less.

5. **One-Color Cheesecloth.** Satin latex paint, glazing medium, pre-laundered cheesecloth. Apply glaze to the wall using a Whizz roller in a 2' × 2' section. Immediately take your bunched cheesecloth and

with a twisting motion tap the wall, firmly blending the color and softening the definition. (See 2-color cheesecloth below.)

Two-Stage Faux Painting Techniques

1. **Dragging, Strie, Flogging, Color Weaving, Stippling, and Spattering.** These painting techniques require a base coat that is applied and then manipulated with a different tool before it dries. The glaze is applied and manipulated while wet with a comb, brush, or stippling brush and is dragged, splattered, flogged, or pounced into the paint to create a unique texture. You will need a satin latex paint, medium glaze, and the tool required for the chosen process. Since a glaze is applied first in a small area (usually an 18" strip), and then a comb or brush is run through it, it is a little more time consuming. I would bid these types of jobs as an hour and a half per 12' × 8' wall section. You must wipe your comb or brush after each swipe so it is a little more labor and time consuming and can be messier. If your lines are not straight, it can also entail some finessing.

2. **Paper Frottage.** Frottage is the art of applying paper to wet glaze to create stone-like effects. You can use ordinary copy-machine paper applied in rows that resembles stone blocks. Lining paper, tissue paper, corrugated paper, craft paper, newspaper, or paper shopping bags can all be used to create beautiful effects. If the base coat color is not what is needed, this will require basecoating the wall first and allowing it to dry. It then becomes a 2-part process. You will need a satin latex paint color, glazing medium and paper in 8 1/2" × 11" sizes or larger. You will apply the glaze in a four-foot-square section and then press your paper of choice into the wet glaze. You will then peel the paper carefully and discard it in a waiting trash receptacle. This can get messy. You can also crumple the paper ahead of time for a more dramatic look. I would allow 1 1/2 to 2 hours per wall (12' × 8') for these techniques.

3. **Pearlescent Paints.** There are wonderful paints today done in a pearly finish that cast a soft shimmer over the wall surface. Pearlescent or

opalescent paint is a transluscent finishing product, much like a glaze that is applied over a base coat. Semigloss latex paint for base coat, pearlescent or opalescent paint, block stippler, and a small stipple brush or stencil brush for edges and corners. Working in a two foot area, apply the glaze then pounce the stippler while glaze is wet. This is time-consuming as you will be applying glaze to small sections, stippling, and repeating the process. Wipe excess paint onto a clean cloth between sections. Allow an hour and a half to two hours for this one.

4. **Two-Color Cheesecloth.** Two colors add more dimension than one. Pre-launder your cheesecloth to remove loose fibers. Use multiple pieces held in a poof ball. Be careful to keep your fingers at the back as they can push through and leave finger markings. Use a Whizz roller and apply the first color glaze to a 2' × 2' wall area, covering about 60 percent of the wall. Immediately apply the second glaze over 60 percent of the area, filling in some of the negative space left by the first roller. Now take your bunched cheesecloth and with a twisting motion, pat the surface firmly to even the glaze. I would allow two hours a wall for this technique.

Three-Stage, Four-Stage, and More Faux Painting Techniques

The following techniques may require more than three steps. You should have an idea now of various stages and set-up requirements. There are amazing books on the market that will show you in a detailed step-by-step format how to render even the most complicated finishes. There is a list of my favorite technique books in the reference section at the end of this book. My intention with this book is to teach you how to start a business and run it successfully. My focus in this chapter is to help you understand how to bid these sometimes time-intensive recipes.

1. **Troweling.** This technique is not to be confused with plaster troweling. This technique uses a number of paint colors applied to the wall with a metal or plastic trowel. Typically you are using a dark, medium, and light palette, applied to the wall with a hand trowel. The wall remains smooth and can be easily repainted at a later date. You will need a flat wall finish for this technique. No base

coat is necessary. To achieve powerful color effects, jewel tones and deep earth tones can be very dramatic. Muted effects can be achieved with softer hues such as pastels or colors tinted with white. Concentrating darker colors along the baseboard and in corners will give the room a worn, vintage look. You will be pouring three or more colors side by side in a pan and dipping a small plastic trowel into them one at a time beginning with the darker color. Apply it to the walls in short random steps, swiping the trowel over the surface in one three-foot area at a time. Repeat these steps with the other colors working from dark to light. This is time consuming, and paint is continuously applied until the desired look is achieved. I would give this technique two hours per 8' × 12' wall section.

2. **Textured Metallic.** Metallic paints have hit the faux painting industry in a big way. Though generally used in isolated areas such as art niches, above fireplaces and cabinets, and perhaps on a focus wall, they are making their debut as full room finishes for a very dramatic effect. Washing a light green latex over copper and/or bronze, creates the look of an aged patina that is so popular today. Due to the use of vinyl spackle in this technique, the drywall would have to be removed if the client ever tires of the finish and wants something else. This is a complex process requiring a basecoat of vinyl spackle applied to the wall and then a sea sponge run through it to make a striated, textured look. It is then basecoated with brown latex paint and allowed to dry. Next the two metallic colors of copper and bronze are applied separately and a final wash of latex green for the patina added. I would allow three hours per wall for this technique unless you are concentrating only on something like a small art niche.

3. **Fresco.** We will cover fresco in the mural section of this chapter as well. Fresco creates a stucco-like appearance. You will be working with a drywall joint compound which dries quickly, so you may want to consider using a partner for this finish. Apply a 1/8" layer of compound to the wall with a spackling knife. Allow it to dry. Sand down high ridges or bumps. Vacuum the wall. Apply drywall primer to the wall surface using a roller. Allow it to dry. Apply the base coat and let dry. Apply the glazing medium in a color wash using a 4" to 6" paintbrush.

As you can see, this technique requires several steps with drying time between each one. Allow your bid to reflect the time needed for each step and the fact that the wall must dry each time, which will mean repeated trips to the location and some downtime. I would bid this as three hours per wall for the plaster, sanding, and vacuuming, one hour for the primer, one hour for the base coat, and an hour and a half for the color wash, making it a five hour per wall bid in total.

4. **Venetian Plaster**. Few techniques have so speedily gained popularity as Venetian Plaster. It is without equal in luster and depth. It has the mellowed, Old World appearance so sought after in today's market. The plasters are sold in tinted hues and applied to the wall with trowels. It is normally a three-part process with dramatic results. Apply a primer and allow it to dry. Apply the first thin coat of plaster to a section of wall using a small trowel. Using a large trowel, smooth out the wall and allow it to dry. Apply a second thin coat in the same manner as above and allow it to dry. Apply a third and final coat using the large trowel, smoothing it over the second layer. Allow it to dry. Sand the wall very lightly with 220-grit sandpaper, then sand it again with 400-grit sandpaper to subtly polish the top coat of plaster. Remove dust with a damp rag.

   This is labor-intensive and I would bid this as two hours per 8' × 12' wall section **per step**, with the exception of wiping it down with a slightly damp rag. That should only take thirty minutes for a wall section that size.

5. **Denim and Linen.** These finishes require basecoating a wall and then applying two latex glazes in different shades of the same color. While the glaze is wet, a brush is dragged through the glaze in two precise patterns: horizontally and vertically, each using a different shade of paint. You will be working from top to bottom on the wall in small sections, always going in the same direction with each shade, i.e., light blue in a horizontal dragging pattern, dark blue in vertical. I would allow one hour per wall for the basecoat, two hours for horizontal dragging, and two hours for vertical dragging. You will need to allow the three steps to dry completely between steps (basecoat, horizontal, vertical applications).

6. **Grasscloth.** Grasscloth wallpaper is an expensive and elegant wall-covering that can be replicated with paint and a squeegee. Sand- and wheat-colored paints will give you a realistic look because they emulate grass colors. Apply a base coat and let dry. With a pencil, mark off three-foot vertical panels around the room using a level for perfectly straight lines. Tape off every other panel. Cut your plastic squeegee with scissors at ¼" apart for each sawtooth section. Fill in the first panel with your top-coat color. Immediately draw the squeegee across the painted surface horizontally, beginning at the top and moving down. Overlap the passes to simulate grass. Wipe the paint from the squeegee after each swipe. Remove the tape before the paint dries. Repeat these steps for each alternating wall section. Allow each section to dry. Tape off the painted sections, positioning the tape 1/8" inside the painted edges. This will give the illusion of seamed wallpaper. Repeat the steps as above for these panels. Remove tape and allow it to dry. Due to the time involved in measuring the room and dividing it into panels, marking it off and taping, applying the basecoat and then the top coat, pulling the squeegee through the wet paint, and repeating these steps (with the exception of the original basecoating step), I would bid this one as follows: one hour for basecoat per wall (8' × 12' wall section); one hour for measuring, marking, and taping; one hour to apply top coat; two hours to pull the squeegee through the panels; thirty minutes to tape alternate panels; one hour to apply top coat; two hours to pull squeegee through the panels. This is a technique that will probably speed up as you do more than one wall, but I would allow the above time increments for your first wall until you get a rhythm going.

7. **Parchment.** Wrinkled tissue paper is sealed into the paint giving the wall a parchment look. Scrunch up whole pieces of tissue paper (enough to cover the wall in a single layer) and set them aside. Basecoat the wall in an area slightly larger than a sheet of tissue paper. While paint is wet, open up a sheet of crumpled tissue paper and apply it to the walls using your hands to smooth it into the wet paint. Do not smooth it out all the way but leave small crinkles

in the paper. Roll over the tissue with a second coat of the base paint, moving carefully so that you don't press down your edges or tear the paper. Repeat these steps for each section, overlapping the papers. Let dry. You can apply a colorwash finish of burnt umber or a light brown if you wish to give it an aged look. Allow an hour per wall for the basecoat, one hour per wall to apply the crumpled tissue paper, one hour to apply the second coat of color. If you apply an antiquing wash, allow another thirty to forty-five minutes. Don't forget to factor in time to crumple the tissue papers.

8. **Suede.** This finish gives the illusion of real suede and is a very rich effect. It has a grainy appearance. Suede-finish latex paint base is available from several paint manufacturers and can be tinted to any color. Earthy colors work best as they resemble real suede: brown, sand, cream, tan, red, cinnamon, clay, and terra cotta are good choices. Apply a tinted primer that matches the topcoat color you've selected. Let dry. Roll paint in a zigzag pattern. Continue down to the next 2' square section and repeat the process until the vertical strip of wall is filled in with paint. Smooth with long vertical strokes. Repeat these steps until the entire wall is painted with the first coat. Allow it to dry. Using a 4" brush, apply a second coat of suede paint in a crosshatch pattern over the entire wall, working from top to bottom, then left to right. This is not a hard finish to render. I would allow one hour for the primer coat per 8' × 12' wall section, one hour to roll on paint in zigzag pattern, and two hours per wall for the time needed for the 4" brush work.

9. **Leather.** The leather glaze technique works best when used with colors that emulate real leather such as burnt sienna, chocolate brown, and slates. For this finish you can use large plastic garbage bags, the sides cut apart with scissors to allow them to lay flat. For a truly authentic leather look, base coat the wall in a lighter shade than the color you've chosen and allow it to dry. Apply the glaze in an area slightly larger than the garbage bag. Smooth a sheet of plastic onto the glaze, scrunching it slightly to allow for a few wrinkles. Peel the plastic from the wall and throw away. Repeat these steps for the adjacent areas. This is not a complicated technique. Allow

the time it takes you to cut apart the garbage bags in your bid. Bid one hour per 8' × 12' wall section for the base coat. Allow another hour per wall for the glazing and one hour for applying and removing the plastic.

10. **Wood Graining.** There are different ways to achieve a wood-grained look (or *faux bois*). This can be done with a tool called a rocker, or by flogging, or brushing through glaze with a 4" painter's brush. In all cases a basecoat is applied, usually in a tone that complements the color you are trying to achieve (honey, mahogany, walnut, pecan, etc.) and allowed to dry. Paint with a topcoat of satin latex paint and while wet, manipulate the paint with your wood graining tools. You will be working in narrow strips, usually the width of a roller, so this is time-consuming for a full wall. Allow three to four hours per wall for a rocker, a little less for flogging and brushing.

11. **Stone Effects.** The market is filled with faux stone effects with everything from fossil rock, granite, and marble, to blocked stone walls and 2-D cement imitations. Granite requires a three-color sponging effect with a splatter finish, while marbling can include up to five colors or more, softened with brushes and highlighted with a feathering technique. Imitation stone blocks require a basecoat, sponging, sometimes frottage effects, measuring, taping off, and oftentimes a splatter effect. Based on the information given above for other faux techniques, figure out the time needed for measuring, taping, sponging, frottage, splatter, etc. Break down each component into time allotments and decide your bidding process based on the hourly wage or daily wage you set. Remember to factor in your time for preparing specialty tools such as crumpled papers, hand-cut squeegees, cut sponges, and fancy brush cuttings. There are hundreds of books out there that will show you step-by-step procedures for today's faux painting techniques, allowing you to figure out the time needed for each step based on the information I have given you in this chapter. I have included my favorite books in the reference section of this book, but of course new books are hitting the stores everyday.

12. **Crackle.** Crackling will give the illusion of timeworn, weathered walls with its effect of hairline cracks in random patterns. Read the manufacturer's label carefully as this is a time-sensitive technique. Apply a base coat to the walls and allow it to dry. Roll the crackle medium onto the walls. Allow the wall to dry according to the manufacturer's instructions (usually thirty minutes). Apply the top coat over the crackle medium, using a wide paintbrush. Allow it to dry. Seal the crackle finish with a sealant recommended by the manufacturer. To bid this job, allow one hour to basecoat each wall, one hour to apply crackle and two hours to apply topcoat with a 6" brush.

Wall Embellishments

Stencils, stamping, reverse stamping, dimensional stenciling, caulking, decoupage, collage, painted tiles, and words are just a few of the many uniquely different wall embellishments. In today's faux painting industry, the number of decorative painting effects you can achieve is limited only by your imagination. Stencils, once a simple, single acetate sheet, are now complex overlays of eight, ten, or more sheets, and have jumped off the wall with textured treatments using caulking, vinyl spackle, embossing mediums, and even bits of costume jewelry, foils, and sand. Decoupage can use fabric, paper, plants, jewelry, and pretty much anything you find laying around the house. It would be impossible for me to break all these down into a bidding process as the steps are as varied as the techniques. Simply use our guidelines above to break down your project into steps, including measuring the room for stencil patterns that repeat, sanding, taping, sealing, cutting, gluing, time to create mosaic motifs, etc.

Ceilings, Floors, Molding, and Doors

Haloed ceilings, metallic paints, skies, Venetian plaster, stamped motifs, faux drapery, graphics, leaf motifs, stencils, faux tin, decorative molding, ceiling medallions and much more constitute the world of ceilings. Elaborate murals are painted on ceilings, both directly onto the surface and rendered on canvas and adhered. Floors can be decorated in stains, cements, stenciling, floor cloths, distressed hardwoods, colored Japanese inlays, faux bois, antiqued brick pavers, stripes, ironwork, and much more.

Moldings can be antiqued, gold-gilded, and faux-boised. Doors can be rendered in faux bois imitating any number of wood grains and even inlaid parquet. They can be finished in stainless steel imitators, murals, frosted glass, imitation stained glass, and stone.

Again, this arena is vast and the time required is based on myriad details. You will need to look at the technique you wish to emulate and break down the steps. An excellent book that shows you the step-by-step processes for all of the techniques included in this chapter is *Decorative Painting Techniques for Walls, Floors, Ceilings, and Furniture* by Elise C. Kinkead and Gail E. McCauley.

Furniture

Faux painting technique for furniture is another widely varied field of effects. The main thing to keep in mind when bidding furniture techniques is the prep time. Rarely will you receive a piece of furniture to work on that doesn't require some kind of preparation prior to applying the paint or rendering a mural or other decorative effects. Varnishes may need to be removed, sanding is usually required, and finally clean-up of the grit with a tack cloth. You may need to remove hardware, tape off drawers and edges, apply a graphic using transfer paper such as graphite paper, measure, align, and factor in elements. The technique itself may require a primer or other basecoat before you actually begin your fancy finish. Today's furniture can be seen with various finishes which include, negoro-uri, montages, intarsia, broken paint, reactive finishes, crackle, faux tiles, parchment, chalkboard paint, stamping, stenciling, magnetic paint, geometric designs, torn paper, striping, decoupage, faux marquetry, faux leather, marble, verdigris patina, lapis, burled wood, rust, copper gilding, noton, antique gold, pickling, trompe l'oeil, gilding, and stained antiquing. The list goes on and on. Again, find a recipe book that shows you step by step how to render the technique and bid your time according to steps. The techniques covered in this chapter should give you a good idea now as to how long it will take you to paint an area. Murals and fancy stencils, lettering and other decorative finishes will need to be carefully calculated as to the time needed to render a quality result.

Murals

The wonderful world of murals is evolving as well. No longer content to have murals remain flatly represented on a wall, artists are adding products to murals that bring them to life. I just returned from Disneyland and ran everywhere taking pictures of murals and architectural elements using everything from cement and fluorescent paint to backlighting, hologram foils, and resins. I was like a kid in a candy store taking it all in.

Sepia toned murals bring back a feeling of nostalgia and yesteryear. With this limited palette you can create amazing depth.

Trompe l'oeil (French for "trick the eye") is a huge field, with everything from fake windows, draperies and doors to floors, stone fountains, stone walls, and much more.

Wood graining is found in murals in the form of doors, trees, barns, etc.

Crackle finishes are also found in murals, giving them an aged, whimsical feel. Used on various parts of animals painted in a mural, they can resemble rawhide or the leathery appearance of faces, arms, legs, and hides.

Canvas murals are gaining in popularity for those clients who want the peace of mind of knowing they can take a mural down when they have tired of it, are moving to another location, or want to move it to another room. Some murals are handed down in families or sold at estate auctions. Make sure you buy pre-treated canvas or use gesso to prime it yourself.

Fresco murals are very popular as they emulate Old World masterpieces. You can use plastering compounds such as PlasterTex by Faux Effects, Rapid-Bond Joint Compound 90 set (drywall powder), vinyl spackle, drywall compound, and, in some cases, cement to create realistic fresco effects of crumbling stone and aged paintings. These are time-consuming techniques and must be bid according to the time needed for mixing the compounds, applying them, sanding, vacuuming, tacking, painting, and sealing when called for.

Stencils are used in murals, both in regular work and frescoes. They can be built up with plasters and vinyl spackle to create wonderful 2-D effects.

Flex-C-Ment Concrete is being used to create very realistic stone facades, trees, walls, etc. Whatever dimension you wish to create can be sculpted from this remarkable cement medium. Walls are now coming to life with elements that extend off the wall in wonderful ways.

Acrylic foil painting is a new creation on the mural circuit. Murals are enhanced in areas that would benefit from shiny metallic surfaces. Space ships and athletes' helmets come to mind. Hologram foil is especially eye-catching. These are sometimes hard to find so search online under "metallic foils" or consult your local interior design facility.

Fluorescent paints used with a black light are wonderful for ceilings and areas where whimsy is appropriate. Galaxies and underwater scenes come to life.

Pearlescent and lusterstone paints add depth and texture to murals. Basically any faux finish can be incorporated into a mural. I have used many faux techniques to enhance my murals.

Sky scenes: A word here about painting skies. You will get asked to paint realistic cloud scenes sometime in your career. Children's bedroom ceilings are especially popular for this. With the use of a simple sponge or something more elaborate such as an airbrush system, clouds can be rendered to look very realistic. Bid these walls based on your equipment, height (I always charge a little extra for ceiling work or areas that require an extension ladder), and amount of wall area. Usually you will need a base coat in day or night sky colors. If painting a night scene where the clouds are more of a backdrop for twinkling stars, keep the cloud detail to a minimum and play up the stars which can be painted in metallics or fluorescent paints.

Accounting for Prep Work and Materials

These are just a few of the techniques used in mural creations. As we've discussed, murals are found everywhere! Take into account prep time. If painting on metal, you may have to prime it, remove rust, etc. Wood may need to be sanded, primed, and sealed. Furniture, as mentioned above, requires a great deal of prep and finishing work. Painting on tiles will require a sealant and perhaps an enamel paint. Glass etching requires acids and other technical products and procedures. Projects that will be out in the elements such as garden creations, boats, cars, and signs will need specialty sealants and appropriate paints.

I hope this section has helped you to narrow down different techniques and to better understand what is required to render them. Your local library or bookstore has books that will inspire you and aid you in step-by-step approaches to your projects.

11

MOTIVATION AND GOALS

Owning your own business brings a feeling of pride and accomplishment. You took a risk . . . a big one, and you're setting up shop. You walked away from the security of a consistent paycheck, paid medical plans, retirement funds, and, possibly, bonuses and commissions.

You also walked away from early-morning commutes, someone telling you when to go to lunch and what time to be back, structured break routines, office gossip, irate bosses, and corporate politics.

Right now, if you are reading this book before diving in, you are probably pretty nervous and wondering if the phone will ring with calls other than from solicitors and friends teasing you about losing your mind. It will! It just takes some hard work and determination to make your dreams, your goals, succeed.

Setting Goals for Your Business

Get out a large yellow legal pad or a few sheets of blank paper. At the top of the paper, write the name of the first month you plan to begin organizing your business—for instance, March. Under "March," make a numbered list of things you'll have to do to move forward. (A To Do Checklist to Get Started is provided in the next chapter for some of these things.)

Include in your list such things as choosing your business name, registering with the state, deciding your advertising budget and what you'll include in that budget, i.e., Yellow Pages, flyers, direct mail, etc. Write down all supplies needed to stock your storage area: ladders, sponges, paints, tarps, etc. How is your office setup? Do you need a fax machine or Rolodex? Have you made arrangements at your bank for your new business checking account?

Write everything down, no matter how trivial, to give yourself a good overview of where you stand in your organization quest. Did you buy a portfolio, a diary, a calculator? Have your business cards been ordered? What about invoices? Are you going to have your vehicle lettered?

As you look down this list, is it within your financial means or will you need a little help getting started? I started my business on $500 thirty-two years ago. I already had a computer, so the main investments were a couple of ladders, business cards, car lettering, and paying the registration fees. I landed my first job, asked for half down, and went out and bought the paint, sponge, and two tarps.

Build slowly. You don't have to buy four ladders right now. Buy a six-foot ladder for now, if money is tight, and wait to see what your first few jobs require. You can rent extension ladders or an elaborate scaffolding setup from a rental company. Buy the paints as needed, as well as glazing mediums, brushes, etc. Put your dollars in advertising right now; you need to generate business first.

If at all possible, try to avoid starting your business in debt. If you feel you need a loan, get a small one. A thousand dollars will cover everything you need and give you a small buffer. This does not include paying your monthly obligations for mortgage, utilities, etc., but, hopefully, you considered those before you told your old boss good-bye.

Once you've checked off your list of necessities to open shop, concentrate on your plan of attack to bring in new clients. On a different sheet of paper, write "Advertising" at the top. Number your page according to how many areas of advertising you feel you can manage financially. Here's a sample:

YELLOW PAGES: Design box ad (1/4 page) and decide listing it will fall under: Interior Decorators, or Painting Contractors, or both. Call Yellow Pages salesperson and discuss rates and deadlines for copy. (Most phone books have a September deadline if you want your ad to run in the new year's edition.) If only ordering a single-line heading, do I want it in bold type? Where should I put my free listing? Under Murals, Painting Contractors, or Artists?

CAR LETTERING: Call sign company and get a bid for car lettering and logo design (if one has not been designed yet) and scan fee if my logo has to be scanned. What is their turnaround time?

FLYERS: Make a dummy copy of a flyer and take it to a copier store to price full-color bordered paper and cost for copies. Decide layout based on where border falls on selected paper, and type up final copy to be printed. Have flyers run off. Deliver flyers to chosen neighborhoods. Hire several young people, if money permits.

DIRECT MAIL: Look up companies under Mailing Services in the Yellow Pages and call for price breakdowns. Ask about turnaround time and distribution areas. Will my ad be thrown in with others or delivered singly? Can I just purchase mailing lists and make my own flyers and handle the postage myself?

COUPON MAILERS: Look up companies under Mailing Services and inquire into costs to include my ad in a mass coupon mailer.

TELEVISION OR RADIO SPOTS: Is my budget large enough to use this media for advertising? What are my area's demographics for potential clients?

NEWSPAPER OR MAGAZINE: Is the expense for newspaper equal to the response rate? Do we have a local magazine targeting my potential client market? Call to get bids on the Classified section for a listing under Services.

You now have goals set to begin acquiring necessary items to legally launch your business, and an advertising agenda that will get you on the road to orders.

Your next goal will be to put together a business plan. How much will you need to earn per month to cover your living expenses, pay your business's taxes, cover supplies, and make a profit? $3,600? $5,000? More? Take some time here to calculate your financial needs and what you realistically think you can charge for jobs. How many do you feel you can land in the first several months of operation? Were you hoping I would tell you that? I can't, but I can give you a guideline based on my experience.

If you distribute one hundred flyers to homes, you can expect to receive one-to-five calls. This may seem low, but it's realistic. One call could mean a $2,000 job and branch-off referrals. Cold-calling on some businesses under construction or in the remodeling process could garner a job within minutes.

When the Yellow Page ad comes out, you will probably receive anywhere from two to ten calls a month if your competition is high. You might receive a lot more calls than this, but I'm giving you an average.

People noticing your car lettering will call an average of once a month.

Newspaper ads are iffy, and some never receive calls for business. I don't deal with direct mail or coupons, although a landscaping friend of mine has had good results with mass coupon mailers. Direct mail could garner several jobs, as most mailers hit at least a thousand homes.

I would continue to distribute flyers to upscale neighborhoods for as long as my budget held out. The more you deliver, the greater your odds for calls. Mention your referral program when you go for the interview to get the ball rolling.

If you feel your financial needs fall somewhere in the $4,000 range for each month's obligations, you will need to land ten jobs paying $400 each. This would mean painting two-and-a-half jobs per week. Since you should average at least $400 a day for a full day's work, you would have three days a week left over to go out and advertise for more jobs.

A good average income in the beginning would be $3,600 a month. After six months, and some good referrals in your pocket, it can easily escalate to $5,000 and $6,000 per month if you're willing to work hard and keep the flyers coming. There are the big jobs that will pay you a five-figure sum by themselves; commercial jobs can bring in as much as $20,000 or more.

Set your goals now for the amount of time you will spend each day in drumming up business. Determine the radius you'd be willing to work inside of, and drive it. Would a thirty-mile range be comfortable to drive to and from a client's location? Then canvas a thirty-mile radius and write down the phone numbers on signs located in front of new buildings going up. Note new subdivisions and the number of homes inside. Check out existing medical facilities and look for walls lacking in luster or murals. Pediatric wings, daycares, and animal clinics are always looking for murals.

Your financial goals will be met strictly by your determination to meet them. Don't be ambiguous here about what you *hope* to make each month. Decide your financial goal and advertise until you meet it, or surpass it.

Lastly, decide where you want to be a year from now. Are you still working alone or are you bringing in help in the form of subcontractors or freelance artists? Have you expanded into an empty room in the basement or opened up shop across town? What do you envision for your new business? This visualization process is all-important. We will talk about it later in this chapter.

Staying Motivated

When you work for yourself, it is sometimes hard to stay motivated on the days when nothing seems to be going right. The excitement you felt in the beginning, as you ran around showing friends your cool new logo and ordering shiny office equipment and outfitting your van, has faded a little as the job of soliciting clients rears its unpredictable head. Your doors are open for business and the phone isn't ringing . . . or it's ringing too much and you are swamped. Everyone wants their sample boards *now*, and the fact that your son just had knee surgery means little.

Your family has decided your new business is more of an inconvenience than blessing to their home sweet home. The children want to use the computer for war games while you're typing up a commercial bid. Your spouse can't find the Christmas ornaments among the gallons of paint lining the basement shelves.

In times like these you wonder if flipping burgers for Fast Jack's wouldn't be a better way to go. This was supposed to be great! The American Dream come true right in the comfort of your loving home.

You know what? It's still great. You're just experiencing what every businessperson goes through. You don't think your old boss didn't have days like this? Every entrepreneur out there worries, stresses, and checks his sanity from day to day. Where you used to have fellow employees around you to beef with and commiserate with, you now hear only your voice whimpering in the dark.

Owning your own business can be lonely sometimes.

Tape over your desk a message with an uplifting expression that motivates you. One of my favorite quotes is from Victor Hugo, "Nothing is as powerful as a dream whose time has come." I also like one by Wayne Dyer, "When you change the way you look at things, the things you look at change."

Have a list of the reasons you wanted to go into business for yourself laminated and propped up against your pencil sharpener. Remind yourself how much you detested working next to Richard Freedman at the office, with his annoying gum-popping and pencil-tapping mannerisms. Remember the timed lunch breaks? The obligatory Christmas parties? See? I sense a smile spreading across your face already. You wanted to try running your own ship and you've done it! Puff up those sails and see where it goes!

The Slump Days

I've noticed something during the many years I've been in business: the year has a rhythm to it when it comes to getting work. There will be times when the phone rings with new jobs every day; sometimes several in one day. Other days may bring only solicitors.

January is usually a slow month. People have spent their money on Christmas and are trying to figure out what they want to achieve themselves for the new year.

February tends to pick up, as people feel the first consciousness of an upcoming spring. They've paid off Christmas bills, begun figuring their taxes, and have decided to shake the cold winter light by adding some color to their homes.

March and April rock. Spring fever kicks in, and everyone is shopping for draperies, throw pillows, and paint. April is one of the two busiest months for me. It's my go-to month for new work and referrals. I am usually booked six months out after March winds down.

May is still strong, and is a great month to drum up work for the summer months.

June, July, and August are unpredictable. Since they are vacation months, it's a toss-up on how many phone calls you'll get. That's why it's smart to load your calendar during the spring rush so you can sail right through the summer months. The upside is that most people receiving tax returns during this time frame are willing to do something fun with it . . . enter their favorite artist.

September picks up again. Once the kids are back in school, moms are rubbing their hands together and looking around for home improvements. A sense of the holidays in the not-too-far-off future begins nibbling at their decorating consciousness.

October is my second time of the year when the phone goes nuts. Everyone wants their homes to look good for the relatives who'll be arriving in the next two months. Most people know to book artists and craftspeople ahead of time for this busy time of year, so October can be counted on to fill your coffers.

November will be busy for the above-mentioned reason.

December tends to slow down on new orders, although you will probably be painting right up until Christmas Eve.

As you can see, the slump days are few if you're smart in your booking and aggressive in going out during the big months of April and October and lining up work that will see you through the summer and winter.

If you fall into a slump period, it helps to ask how other businesses are doing; not just in the painting industry. I guarantee, they will tell you they are experiencing the same slowdown in traffic. It's strange, but, like I said earlier, the year tends to have its own rhythm. Worrying about it will only make you nervous.

During the slow times, create a new and exciting flyer offering a seasonal special. People can't resist discounts and specials. Offer a package deal on rooms to be painted, or run a children's mural offer. Getting off your palette and getting out in the sunshine will do more for you than anything else. Knowing you are doing something positive to promote business will perk up your spirits.

Network when things are slow. Go to lunch with other entrepreneurs and brainstorm! This is a magic elixir for the blues. You will come back to your studio pumped with new ideas and enthusiasm. It only takes one person to tell you how great you are and how they envy your talent or business to get you soaring in the entrepreneurial heavens again.

One thing that always gets my creative juices flowing is to go to bookstores and look at all the latest books on murals and faux painting techniques. I also look at interior decorating books and magazines and I can feel a renewed stirring of enthusiasm. If there is a home show going on nearby, attend it and soak up all the new ideas in décor and wall finishes. Go to home and garden expos or wander through the aisles of craft and hobby stores. I guarantee you come back inspired, perhaps with new ideas to put on a brand new flyer!

Join organizations around town geared to home-based business owners. Your chamber of commerce will have a list. Hobnobbing with others who have hung out their shingles is uplifting and a great way to bring in new business. The Passing of the Cards is a time-honored tradition at these meetings.

Drive around and look for new work. Grab a cold soft drink at the drive-thru, set your notepad and pencil in the seat next to you, and cruise the thirty-mile area you set up for yourself. Again, getting outside and doing something to bring in new work will invigorate you during the slump times.

Finally, remind yourself how blessed you are to have a talent in demand enough to warrant creating a business just for it. Not everyone can take their skills and market them in a way that puts food on the table. Faux finishing and murals is one market where the money potential is incredible. Then, you get the added perk of the mind-blowing praise that artists tend to receive. There are people out there who go to work every day of their lives and the only attention they receive is when they screw up.

The slump days happen to all of us. Keep it in perspective and work even harder to bring in the new business. Even then, the phone may not ring for a while. It happens. It's that rhythm again. Sail through it with optimism. When it hits the upswing, you'll be up to your eyeballs!

I hope you don't mind if I illustrate this point with a very personal experience. I mentioned in the chapter on murals that the recession of 2008 brought my business to an abrupt halt. Spending large amounts of money for murals and faux painting was not something consumers were willing to do as the economy went spiraling downward and the stock market had more thrills and chills than a carnival roller coaster ride.

It was also during this particular year, 2008, that my personal world fell apart. In a mere eight months I lost my beloved mother, my sister-in-law whom I adored, a grandchild, a favorite aunt, and a Siberian Husky who had been in our family for nine years. A rare tornado ripped through the small town of Windsor, Colorado where I was living and took out most of the windows in my townhome while I stood in the middle of the thundering noise, crying and wondering what was going on. Houses two blocks over were totally destroyed. A four-year relationship I had with a gentleman came to an end, and I got to the point where I was afraid to come out from under the covers in the morning. It was the blackest period of my life. For six months I tried to get my life back, and went back to applying for any job I could get my hands on. I wondered if I would ever recover the lifestyle I had become accustomed to and I missed my mother terribly. She had always been my biggest supporter and fan. I leaned heavily on my family, friends, and my Heavenly Father.

My love of quantum physics enabled me to hold onto the scientific quote that any organism that expands must first hit rock bottom. To be catapulted into the stratosphere, you must first be brought to the point of almost utter destruction. At this point, the organism will either die or explode into areas unimaginable! I read those quotes daily. And on some subliminal level I knew something amazing was coming. I knew I was learning lessons from all the hardships that would serve me well in the future and turn me into a better human being. And guess what? It hit ... and it hit BIG! Like a dam breaking and the water pouring out in torrents, it all hit. In one month's time I was signed up to do five large medical clinics across the United States in murals that would take five to six weeks each, I signed two book contracts in four days, and have since signed another one with a promise for more work in the same genre, my family is thriving, and I have never been happier. People have come into my life that are nurturing, supportive, and passionate about life. I am so much stronger and much more able to take the bumps in the road with a smile and patience than I was ever able to before. The rough times always come with a gift in their hand!

Please remember, when your life is at its darkest, something amazing is about to happen! And those tough times are the character builders that give you new tools that are so much more valuable than the ones you acquire when things are sailing smoothly. I promise!

Being Your Own Fan Club

Just a few words here about your support group. There will be times when your friends and family are less than flag-waving when it comes to your new venture.

People. . . all people. . . tend to feel a little threatened when one of their flock ventures out into the unknown and dares to try something brave. For some, the person doing the venturing is holding up a hypothetical mirror reflecting their own fear of trying something daring themselves. Watching someone else succeed in a new arena is tricky. You have to have a lot of healthy self-esteem to be truly happy for them.

If close friends and family are the ones holding the sour grapes, it may come as a shock. Why aren't they happy for you? They may fear your new job will require a lot of your time; time that was once reserved for them. Perhaps the feeling of seeing you soar off into the unknown leaves them a little nervous. Will you be the same old Harvey who bowls with them on Saturday nights?

Success brings out a lot of different emotions in people around you; some great, some disheartening. Try not to judge the ones who are acting strangely too harshly. It may be their own inadequacies they are feeling. Give them time to get used to the new you, and they'll come around. If your business goes through the roof, however, it may only get worse. Unfortunately, it is times like these that determine who your true friends are.

Tune up now for your one-man orchestra. Remember, "the one who leads the orchestra must turn her back to the crowd." If you can be proud of yourself regardless of others' good or ill will, you will never have a bad day. Be happy for their successes and keep your feet on the ground when things are going well for you.

Appreciate what you've been given. This outlook of going through each day grateful for the talent that enables you to earn a living will see you through and continue to bring abundance into your life. Be your own fan club.

The Power of Positive Projection

If you don't believe in the power of positive thinking and the impact it can have in your life, you may skip this final section.

For me, and millions of others, the ability to project positive images and visualize a preferred outcome is incredibly powerful. Once you've experienced it, you won't ever go back to letting life buffet you around. It is an incredible feeling to take control of your life and design the outcome you want to see manifest itself.

Years ago, I came up with this brilliant idea of creating a Halloween carnival, complete with custom-made midway games and spooky prizes. I spent weeks drawing the characters and creating challenging games with names such as Waste the Werewolf, Ghosts Night Out, and Dunk Dracula.

I priced a huge big-top tent, located a great site next to a thriving grocery store, and estimated radio spot costs and other advertising. Everything was working. I went to bed every night visualizing the carnival. Every detail was formed in my mind, right down to the location for the cotton candy machine and the spotlight in the parking lot.

Things began to happen. The owner of the big-top tent said he would wait until the carnival closed to collect the tent fee, when his usual procedure was to get half down. The radio gave me a huge discount since I did the spots myself, in my best *Wizard of Oz* witch voice. Vendors chipped in merchandise, the grocery store next to us went in on the cost for the spotlight.

Then, everything came to a halt. When I called the toy company for a final quote on the prizes, I was told the cost, with shipping, came to $12,000! That was $12,000 more than I had. I slumped into a chair and watched my vision of a Halloween carnival filter into dust particles at my feet.

With a heavy heart, I picked up the phone and called the grocery store owner to tell him the carnival would have to wait until next year. I apologized for not being more professional in getting all the costs up front before bringing him in on my enthusiasm for the project. Since the store owned the adjacent lot where the tent was to be set up, I had promised them a percentage of the proceeds. He asked how much the prizes came to. When I told him it was $12,000, he said, "I'll pay for it." It took me several seconds to recover, before I asked him to repeat what he'd just said. "I'll pay for it with my personal credit card," he repeated mildly.

I'm ashamed to say, but any last vestiges of business-like appearance crumbled, as I broke into tears. "You don't even know me," I whimpered. "I think I'm a pretty good judge of character," he replied. "What you've shown me is fun, and I think we'll get a good turnout."

The tent went up, the vendors came, the local radio station did a live remote out front and . . . the people came! For three weeks they came, and the comments were wonderful. As I looked around the tent, I got goose bumps. It was exactly as I had envisioned it every night before I went to sleep. Every game, haunted-tree setup, vendor placement . . . everything. The tent was the exact size needed to hold all thirteen games, the ticket booth, and food carts.

Many times in my life, this process has worked for me. Visualizing your dreams and packing them with detail and enthusiasm is as good as money in the bank in fulfilling those dreams. I won't bore you with the dozens of things that have materialized in my life due to my belief in positive projection, but I know it works. There are hundreds of books out there on this incredible force.

Dr. Wayne Dyer has several I've read, and they always inspire me.

Try it. Find a quiet place and take some deep breaths. Now, relax and begin to envision your own business. See it all, right down to where the pencil holder will sit on your desk. What does your car lettering look like? Your business-card logo? Do you see yourself depositing those checks and the phone ringing with calls from people who loved your work and want you to bid their home or business?

If you've been wanting a larger home or new car, this new business of yours is a means to acquiring those things, so include them in your vision of success.

Spend several minutes every day going over your dream. Feel enthusiasm while you're picturing your new business and all the clients lined up. The key here is to visualize it as it's already manifesting itself in your life . . . not down the road. Be grateful now that this is happening in your life. Don't use future tense when you talk or think about your painting career. Say, "I am so grateful that this is happening now in my life. I am generating business now. People are calling and wanting my work. I go out every day and put plans into action that will guarantee more business. I treat my clients with appreciation and do the very best I can on their projects. I am living my dream . . . right *now*!"

This has brought my dreams into reality so many times that my sons and husband no longer doubt it and are using visualization in their lives. If you go out each day expecting good things to happen . . . they will. Negative thoughts carry just as much weight, so dump them. You don't want negative thinking as your business partner. It will sink you as surely as someone ripping off your business.

Last year I tried this little test at Christmas time. My older sons were teasing me when I came home from shopping one day and told them that prime parking spaces kept opening up for me everywhere I went in overcrowded parking lots. "Sure, Mom. How much eggnog did you have?" were the typical comments.

As the weeks went by, I continued going throughout town, saying, "I would like a parking space, please." Every single time one would open up right in front of the main entrance just as I got there. Several times I had to hit the brakes as someone pulled out in front of me just as I arrived . . . right in front of the store's door! When my sons witnessed this on more than one occasion in a packed mall parking lot, they quit teasing me. Now my husband tells them to go get me during Christmas shopping outings so that we can park close to the store!

There's nothing magic about it . . . in the fairy-dust meaning of the word. I believe it comes from a calm belief that if you put out positive vibes, good things happen. Even when concerned with unimportant parking spaces.

Staying positive about your business will see your sign still hanging over your door when others have packed theirs away and are moving on to the next dream. Believing in your ability and sticking with it in the slow times will assure your success more than expensive equipment and designer briefcases. This is one business that is not a flash in the pan! Faux painting and murals will continue to grow in popularity and technique. The only excuse you can give in this industry for failure is not putting in the effort to continuously grow and learn and failing to always put your client first!

You know people who have talent, but they are too frightened to put their egos on the line and go for it. Years go by, and they are still thinking "what if" and looking longingly at someone else's success. Failure is not the worst thing that can happen to you. The worst thing is not even giving those dreams of yours a sporting chance.

I'm off my soapbox now. I just wanted you to know some of the guidelines to creating a successful faux finishing or mural business. It is entirely obtainable and having a strong belief in yourself is the first thing you should pack in that craft tote of yours.

Best wishes on your new venture. Here's hoping all your clothes are paint-spattered ones!

12

USEFUL FORMS

Some samples of layouts and forms have been scattered throughout the book. Here you'll find a collection of contracts, lists, and worksheets geared to helping you get organized and understand the business of faux finishing, murals, and decorative painting.

These pages are simply a guide; nothing is carved in stone. Put your own wordage or twist into any of these ideas and make them your own. Other forms can be found in Google on the Internet, simply by typing the keywords for worksheets or forms you're looking for. The Web search "Faux Painting" brings up no less than 81,000 referents. Most of these Web sites relate to painting techniques and workshops available throughout the world.

The following pages have been typeset separately, allowing you to photocopy the ones you're interested in.

Sample Contract for Faux Painting: Residential

FE FI FAUX FUM PAINTING

3225 Nantucket Way

Waldorf, Maryland 56012

(555) 983-2406

March 2, 2004

Mr. and Mrs. Client:

Thank you for hiring Fe Fi Faux Fum Painting to render the following glazes and/ or mural work in your home:

Glazes in satin finish for the following areas:

- Kitchen area including dinette. Sherwin Williams Terra Cotta Brick will be glazed on in two layers with a sponge. We will remove cornice over dinette window. All other wall hangings, furnishings, etc. will be removed by owner before work begins.
- Great room and entryway. Sherwin Williams Barely Buff will be glazed in these areas in a one-step color wash with a sponge. Hallway to the left of entry will not be included in this bid as stipulated in attached drawing.
- Guest Bath/Main Floor. Torn paper technique in metallic bronze and burnt umber. Three coats of polyurethane will be added to the completed wall treatment. Owners are responsible for removal of large gold-gilt mirror before arrival.

You and the interior designer will please initial the color selections mentioned above and corresponding techniques chosen. Sample boards have been initialed by both you and the interior decorating firm.

If any add-ons or changes are incurred during the completion of this project, the fee stated in the invoice will be altered to reflect these changes.

You have agreed to removal of all furnishings, accessories, and throw rugs in these three areas prior to our arrival.

You have stipulated the laundry room as the area we may use for clean-up and as our water source.

As discussed, we will leave our paints, tools and equipment in the garage to the left of the freezer. You have supplied us with a keypad combination to the garage door for our use while painting your home. Combination is _____.

Wall repairs stipulated during walk-through will be taken care of by you and a twenty-four-hour cure time will have elapsed before our start date.

Any damage done to the walls, other than by our crew, with the exception of minor scratches covered in the free touch-up clause, will incur a repair charge to be determined based on the extent of damage.

Free touch-up clause: Our firm will touch up any minor scratches for the period of one year, free of charge. Dents, large scrapes, permanent marker, crayon, or major damage do not fall under this clause, and a bid will be issued to cover necessary repairs.

Our workers carry liability insurance and workman's compensation.

We have permission to photograph our work and will obtain permission from you to use those photographs for publishing purposes.

You have agreed to have the two dogs kept in the back yard during our project dates, to avoid mishaps or injury.

We are to exit through garage door and close it behind us, using the combination code.

Deposit: The total amount for this project is $2,250. A half-down deposit of $1,125 was given at the time of this contract on March 2, 2004.

If a refund is requested before March 30, 2004, it will be refunded in full. If a refund is requested after that date but before our start date of June 12, 2004, $1,000 will be deducted from the deposit.

The final balance of $2,250 will be due on the completion date of June 24, 2004.

If payment has not been received within 10 days of completion, a 10% interest charge will be added to payment.

Any add-ons could be handled as a separate invoice.

We agree to the above-stipulated conditions.

Artist, Fe Fi Faux Fum Painting Company   Date _____

Mr. and Mrs. Client   Date _____

Residential Sketch for _____
                                          Client's name

Family Room
   Walls A, B, & C fauxed in color-washed Terra Cotta
   Do not continue faux onto Wall D

Sample Contract for Faux Painting: Commercial

FE FI FAUX FUM PAINTING

3225 Nantucket Way

Waldorf, Maryland 56012

(555) 983-2406

November 4, 2004

Business owner:

Thank you for hiring Fe Fi Faux Fum Painting for the recent remodel of your pediatrics clinic at 5690 Mountain Vista Drive in Waldorf, Maryland.

We have scheduled your project to begin on January 4, 2011 and be completed by February 11, 2011. The following services have been requested:

- Faux finishing in waiting area, hallways, receptionist area, five treatment rooms, numbers 1-5 in the west wing of the building and the public restrooms. Faux finish is to be rendered in ICI Forest Stone in a skip-trowel imitation in Italian plaster. Accompanying sketch shows walls to be painted.
- Large mural measuring 8' × 15' × 8' high will be rendered on east wall of waiting area. Sketches of whale scene have been approved and initialed. Furniture directly below mural will be removed by your staff before start date.
- Decorative vines will be stenciled over receptionist's area, trailing over cabinets and filing systems in sage green.

We have been asked to faux finish the walls during morning hours of 7:30 A.M. to 10:30 A.M. and during evening hours of 5:30 P.M. to 9:30 P.M. to reduce interference with clientele. Additional charges have accrued due to unusual work hours.

Our ladders and supplies are to be stored in supply room 1-A in east wing by coat rack. We have been given permission to use small refrigerator in that area. We have been given permission to use the sink in the break room as our water source and for clean-up.

All trim work will be taped off, and tape removed between each work section.

We are to park in the rear by telephone pole and use back door on east side. A key has been provided and will be returned at completion of project.

The project total is $6,000, and a deposit of $3,000 was received on November 4, 2010. Check #_____. The balance of $3,000 is due on completion of project on February 11, 2011. If monies have not been received after 10 business days, a 10% interest rate will be added. If a refund is requested within 30 days of this contract, November 4, 2010, deposit will be refunded in full. Anytime after that date and before project start date, January 4, 2011, $1,000 will be deducted from deposit.

Mainstream Construction will have completed their remodel by January 2, 2010. Any delays on their behalf will be reported to us immediately. The foreman to contact is Mike Hangraves @ (555) 491-9876. If we are delayed beginning our part of the project due to construction delays, a 10% surcharge will be added. If my company cannot begin work on the designated date because the work area is not in proper working condition or the clients are not available, we retain the option to reschedule or charge the client a penalty as described above. Any damage done to our finished wall treatments from construction damage will incur additional charges for repair.

If we have not completed our responsibilities within five days of stated deadline above, barring construction delays, client delays, additional work added, or other factors outside our control, final payment will be reduced by $1,000.

If for any reason the project is terminated due to causes other than dissatisfaction with our company, no refund will be forthcoming and the work completed will be paid for, plus 25%.

We have permission to photograph our work and will obtain permission from you to use those photographs for publishing purposes.

A copy of our Liability and Workman's Compensation Certificates of Insurance are attached.

We agree to the stipulations stated above.

Artist, Fe Fi Faux Fum Painting Company   Date _____

Business Owner(s)   Date _____

Commercial Sketch for _____
Client's name

Waiting Room Area
Walls A, B, C	Sea-Foam Fantasy 2-tone Sponge
Wall E	Marine Color Wash
Wall D	Aquatic mural – continues behind receptionist
Wall F	No

Client Invoice

FE FI FAUX FUM PAINTING

Waldorf, Maryland

(555) 983-2406

Client's name_____   Project Start Date:_____

Client's Address_____   Project Completion Date_____

Client's Phone_____

Description	Technique	Paint Color	Price ----------
Kitchen/Dinette	Ragged/2 Glaze	Burmese Blue #2109 SW	$ 980
Lydia's Room	Mural/Horses	Avoid yellows	1200
Lydia's Dresser	Distressed/roses	Dusky rose over linen wash	400
Project Total:			$2580
Supply Total:			120
Final Total:			$2700
Deposit of Half-Down: $1350 Check # 2343 4/23/2004 _____ (initials)			
Balance Due:	$1350	5/09/2004	
Special requests: Cat is not to be let outside. She will be contained in back guest room. Front door will be left open and we are to lock it behind us on the way out.			
Thank you!			

(signature)

Master List of Materials, Supplies, and Equipment

Client's name_____   Date of Job_____

Address_____   Job Technique_____

Phone_____   Special Requests_____

- ☐ Sandpaper
- ☐ Steel wool
- ☐ Tack cloth
- ☐ Glue
- ☐ Spackle
- ☐ Putty knife
- ☐ Allen wrench set
- ☐ Screwdriver
- ☐ Plastic bucket(s)
- ☐ Powdered drywall mix
- ☐ Plastic sandwich bags
- ☐ Caulk
- ☐ Caulk gun
- ☐ Dust masks
- ☐ Blank sample boards
- ☐ Fine-point permanent markers
- ☐ Hair dryer
- ☐ Quart cans & lids
- ☐ Gallon cans & lids
- ☐ Empty jars with lids
- ☐ Straining cloths
- ☐ Rubber bands
- ☐ Large paper cups
- ☐ Wood sticks
- ☐ House paints
- ☐ Japan colors
- ☐ Tempera paints
- ☐ Acrylic paints
- ☐ Stains
- ☐ Glazing medium

- ☐ Water-base urethane
- ☐ Paint thinner
- ☐ Water
- ☐ Denatured alcohol
- ☐ Graph paper
- ☐ Markers
- ☐ Pencils
- ☐ Pens
- ☐ T-square
- ☐ Ruler
- ☐ Yardstick
- ☐ Measuring tape
- ☐ Templates
- ☐ Paint rollers
- ☐ Paint trays
- ☐ Roller extension
- ☐ Combs
- ☐ Feathers
- ☐ Sponges (synthetic & natural)
- ☐ Chamois
- ☐ Plastic garbage bags
- ☐ Rags
- ☐ Newspaper
- ☐ Erasers
- ☐ Paper napkins
- ☐ Paper towels
- ☐ Cheesecloth
- ☐ Foam brushes (1", 2" & 3")
- ☐ Stencil brushes
- ☐ Filbert brushes
- ☐ Blending brush
- ☐ Artist's brushes
- ☐ Fan brushes
- ☐ Stipple brush
- ☐ Toothbrushes

- ☐ Flogger
- ☐ Masking tape
- ☐ Painter's tape
- ☐ X-ACTO blade
- ☐ Palette knife
- ☐ Single-edge razor blades
- ☐ Scissors
- ☐ Ladders
- ☐ Bucket hooks
- ☐ Collapsible worktable
- ☐ Drop cloths
- ☐ Painter's plastic sheeting
- ☐ Tracing paper
- ☐ Masking fluid or frisket
- ☐ Clear acetate
- ☐ Sketch pad
- ☐ White chalk
- ☐ Colored chalk
- ☐ Transfer paper
- ☐ Specialty compounds such as Flex-C-Ment, If needed
- ☐ Kneepads
- ☐ Folding chair
- ☐ Walmart plastic 3-drawer cart on wheels

Personal items for the job site:

- ☐ Food
- ☐ Water
- ☐ Radio or CD player
- ☐ Soap
- ☐ Hand cleaner
- ☐ Plastic gloves
- ☐ Apron with pockets
- ☐ Work clothes
- ☐ Extra bucket of water if none is available on site
- ☐ Toilet paper if it is new construction

Client-Related Items:

☐ Business cards

☐ Portfolio

☐ Samples

☐ Fan deck of paint colors

☐ Thank-you notes

☐ Thank-you gift

Yellow Page Ad Ideas

Below are two examples of layouts for ads in the Yellow Pages. At top is a full-color ad rendered here in grayscale. The frame is lime green, the company name is hot pink, the telephone number is baby blue, and the image of the display kit represents a wide array of colors. The rest of the type would appear in black. You'll notice that the black-and-white ad on the bottom does not rely on shades of gray to enhance its visual appeal. The black silhouettes of brush and paint enliven the information disclosed and reveal an elegant, playful characteristic about the company.

Glazed Over!

Faux Finishes * Murals
Stencils * Decorative
Painting

Call (555) 345-9876

Free In-Home Estimates

Full-color ad

Black-n-White
Ad

Walls of Fame

Murals . Faux .
Stencils
Hand-Painted Screens &
Furniture

15 years experience
Residential . Commercial

(555) 786-4444

Record-Keeping Charts

Daily Accounting Ledger

Daily Accounting Ledger					Week:			
	Monday	Tuesday	Wednesday	Thursday	Friday	Saturday	Sunday
Income								
Total								
Expenses								
Rent								
Electricity								
Phone								
Debt Payments								
Advertising								
Freelance								
Maintenance								
Supplies/ Office								
Paint Supplies								
Gas								
Other								
Total								
Profit								
Cumulative Profit								

Weekly Accounting Ledger

Weekly Accounting Ledger				Month:	
	Week 1	Week 2	Week 3	Week 4	Week 5
Income					
Total					
Expenses					
Rent					
Electricity					
Phone					
Debt Payments					
Advertising					
Freelance					
Maintenance					
Supplies/ Office					
Paint Supplies					
Gas					
Other					
Total					
Profit					
Cumulative Profit					

Monthly Accounting Ledger

Monthly Accounting Ledger									Year:			
	Jan	Feb.	Mar.	Apr.	May	Jun	Jul	Aug.	Sept.	Oct.	Nov.	Dec.
Income												
Total												
Expenses												
Rent												
Electricity												
Phone												
Debt Payments												
Advertising												
Freelance												
Maintenance												
Supplies/ Office												
Paint Supplies												
Gas												
Other												
Total												
Profit												
Cumulative Profit												

Profit and Loss Records

Profit and Loss Records									Year:			
	Jan.	Feb.	Mar.	Apr.	May	Jun.	Jul.	Aug.	Sept.	Oct.	Nov.	Dec.
Income												
Total												
Expenses												
Rent												
Electricity												
Phone												
Debt Payments												
Advertising												
Freelance												
Maintenance												
Supplies/ Office												
Paint Supplies												
Gas												
Other												
Total												
Profit												
Cumulative Profit												

To Do Checklist to Get Started

☐ Register your name with your state's Department of Revenue.

☐ Obtain your quarterly income tax forms.

☐ Buy insurances for business: liability, personal property, etc.

☐ Have business cards printed up.

☐ Buy or create invoices in two- or three-part carbon sets.

☐ Take your vehicle in to be lettered.

☐ Buy your Professional Trio: briefcase or carrying tote, sample board binder, and photo album.

☐ Buy plastic craft tote for all your small supplies.

☐ Buy ladders, tarps, fauxing tools (sponges, rags, chamois, etc.), tape, paint shields, buckets, trays, foam brushes, pencils, rulers, sandpaper, etc.

☐ Set up an account with your favorite paint store(s) and request a fan deck of colors.

☐ Set up your answering machine or get voice messaging for your phone.

☐ Buy a cell phone if you don't already have one.

☐ Organize your car with paint-can crates, dividers, and storage boxes.

☐ Create your flyers or direct-mail layouts.

☐ Order your Yellow Pages ad.

☐ Check wardrobe for old paint clothes and professional business attire.

☐ Set up your office with computer, fax, copier, and printer; set up files.

Checklist for Interviews
Professional Trio: Briefcase, Sample-Board Binder, and Photo Album
Inside Briefcase

☐ Calculator

☐ Pens, pencils, paper clips

☐ Calendar or diary

☐ Business cards

☐ Invoices

☐ Sample magazine photos or faux books w/ room technique selections

☐ Envelopes to put paint chips, fabric samples, and client's photos in

☐ Measuring tape

☐ Notepads

☐ Books with illustrations of themes client mentioned over the phone

☐ Stencil borders and themes

☐ Client's address and phone number

☐ Cell phone

☐ Optional: diversions for children, such as coloring books or puzzles

Goal Questionnaire
Office Setup:

1. Do I want to work out of my home or a small shop?

2. Where will I work at home? The basement? Study? Garage?

3. Will I be happy if my family and their routine is part of my business environment?

4. Do I have the room for supplies, samples, books, office equipment, etc.?

5. Can I provide an air of professionalism working from this site? What about phone calls and background noise?

Car Setup:

1. Is my car big enough to haul supplies and ladders?

2. Does it lend itself to a professional image?

3. Do I need to add additional coverage now that it's a work vehicle?

Business Structure:

1. Do I want to work alone or bring in a partner?

2. Do I see myself expanding down the road with employees and bigger office space?

3. How would I feel about freelance artists and subcontractors taking care of my clients?

4. Do I want to work on commercial projects, or would the visibility and noise bother me?

5. Is this a career I could build upon and pass along to my children as a family business?

6. Can I create financial security with this type of business structure?

Time:

1. How busy do I want to be?

2. Do I see this as something I'll want to be doing five years from now? Ten? Twenty?

3. Do I want to give up my evenings and occasional weekends?

4. Am I disciplined enough to get up and get going without a time clock waiting for me?

5. Can I make the time and be aggressive about my advertising to keep my calendar filled?

Motivation:

1. Can I pick myself up and keep going on the slump days without a support group?

2. Will carting the same ladders and supplies in and out of job sites year after year take its toll on me? What about negative clients?

3. Can I switch from a noisy workplace with people around to solitary entrepreneurship?

4. Can I put my client's needs above my own once I've accepted their deposit?

RESOURCES AND WORKSHOPS

Books

Decorative Painting for the Home by Lee Andre and David Lipe (Lark Books, 1994)

Decorative Painting Step-by-Step by Better Homes and Gardens (Better Homes and Gardens, 2005)

Paint Effects and Spectacular Finishes: A Simple-to Use Practical Guide for Every Home by Sacha Cohen (Lorenz Books, 2007)

Recipes for Surfaces: Decorative Paint Finishes Made Simple by Mindy Drucker and Pierre Finkelstein (Fireside, 1990)

How to Start Making Money with Your Decorative Painting by Dorothy Egan (North Light Books, 1998)

Easy Fresco by Lina Ferrara (Sterling, 2008)

New Faux Finishes by H. John Johnsen (Sterling, 2001)

Ortho's All About Decorative Painting edited by Larry Johnston (Ortho, 2002)

50 Ways to Paint Ceilings and Floors: The Easy Step-by-Step Way to Decorator Looks by Elise C. Kinkead (Creative Publishing International, 2008)

Decorative Painting Techniques for Walls, Floors, Ceilings, and Furniture by Elise C. Kinkead and Gail E. McCauley (Creative Publishing International, 2009)

Step-by-Step Decorative Painting by Peter and Paula Knott (Meredith Books, 1997)

It's Faux Easy by Gary Lord (North Light Books, 2004)

Mural Painting Secrets for Success: Expert Advice for Hobbyists and Pros by Gary Lord (North Light Books, 2008)

Professional Painted Finishes: A Guide to the Art and Business of Decorative Painting by Ina Brosseau Marx, Allen Marx, and Robert Marx (Watson-Guptill, 1991)

Fabulous Finishes for Your Home: Step by Step by Karl-Heinz Meschbach (North Light Books, 1999)

Faux Finishing for the First Time by Rhonda Rainey (Sterling/Chapelle, 2000)

Decorative Painting and Faux Finishes by Sharon Ross and Elise Kinkead (Creative Homeowner, 2004)

Decorative Paint & Faux Finishes edited by Linda J. Selden and Carol Spier (Sunset Books, 1999)

Fresh Paint: Fun and Easy Ways to Decorate Your Home by Glenwood Sherry (KQED Books, 1997)

The Paint Effects Bible: 100 Recipes for Faux Finishes by Kerry Skinner (Firefly Books, 2003)

Classic Paints and Faux Finishes by Annie Sloan and Kate Gwynn (Readers Digest, 2000)

Magazines

American Artist

AmericanStyle Magazine

Architectural Digest

The Artist's Magazine

ARTnews

Art Times

Better Homes and Gardens

Coastal Living

Dream House Magazine

Kitchens & Bathrooms Quarterly

Luxury Kitchens & Bathrooms

Romantic Homes

Southwest Art

This Old House Magazine

Unique Homes

Watercolor

Wildlife Art

Trade Journals

Airbrush Action Magazine

Architectural Record

Art Calendar Magazine

Art Materials Retailer

HOW Magazine

Interior Landscape Business Magazine

Watercolor Artist

Workshops for Faux Painting

The Faux Finishing School. Run by Martin Allan Hirsch and recognized as one of the best in the nation, this school offers everything to the beginner, intermediate, and advanced artist. A full range of supplies, books, and other services are offered. *www.fauxfinish.com/FauxFinish/mahclass.htm*

Faux Masters Studio. Faux painting classes, workshops, training, and more. Visit their new blog dedicated to faux painting and faux finishing. Network, share, discuss, ask questions, research, learn, find out about the latest events, etc. *www.fauxmasters.com*

Cloud 9 Living Faux Painting Workshop in Austin, Tex. Move your artistic expressions from the canvas on your easel to the walls of your home after this class on Faux Finishing. *www.cloud9living.com/experience-gifts/austin/fauxpainting-workshop*

Donna's Designs. Enjoy a week of creative and professional workshops taught in a non-intimidating atmosphere, combining business and artistic know-how, all for $1,100. *www.learnfaux.com*

Faux Painting Workshops. Snow college in Utah features classes and workshops taught by faux painting expert instructor Regina Garner. *www.snow.edu*

Workshops for Murals

Faux Finishing Schools and Mural Painting Classes

www.trompe-l-oeil-art.com/faux-schools.html

Faux Painting School Classes for Faux Finishing, Trompe L'oeil, and Murals

decartctr.tripod.com

Trompe L'oeil Mural Perspective Workshop. The Faux Finish School offers five-day, hands-on mural painting workshops.

www.fauxfinish.com

MuralPro.com. The Atlanta-based company offers faux and mural workshops and classes.

www.muralpro.com

Contemporary Fresco Painting Resource Center. Nationwide fresco painting workshops.

www.truefresco.com

Muralsplus. A faux painting, murals, and faux finishing question and answer resource with a faux painting and murals information library and a message board. Features new products, workshops, etc.

www.muralsplus.com

The Fresco School. A Los Angeles-based buon fresco painting program featuring mural painting seminars, fresco restoration, and more.

www.frescoschool.org

These are just a few of the workshops being offered around the world as this fascinating industry continues to expand.

Internet Resources

By typing the keywords "faux painting" or "murals" into your Web browser, you will find more sites with information on the latest trends in faux painting and murals than you can possibly browse. Many of these Web sites feature blogs, message boards, tips, step-by-step instruction, products, books, and links to other sites offering even more information. If you are looking for something specific, such as cement staining techniques, simply type that phrase into your browser. Today's technology offers so many wonderful features that are literally at your fingertips. If you are interested in finding additional trade journals or magazines, simply type in "faux painting magazines," sit back, and enjoy.

Index

U
utilities, 33

V
vehicle lettering, 12, 183
  cost of, 11
Venetian Plaster, 172
ventilation, 114
video stores, 46
visualization, 191–192

W
walls
  assessing, 88–89
  base-painted, 105
  embellishments, 176
  height of, 96
  repair, 96
  surfaces of, 105–106
  texture of, 80, 96
water
  buckets of, 109
  sources of, 97
window shades, murals on, 140
wood
  graining, 175, 178
  preparing surface of, 166
work area, 21–22

X
X ACTO blades, 157

Y
Yellow Pages, 9, 182, 184
  advertising ideas, 207

Books from Allworth Press

Allworth Press is an imprint of Allworth Communications, Inc. Selected titles are listed below.

The Business of Being an Artist, Fourth Edition
by Daniel Grant (6 × 9, 408 pages, paperback, $27.50)

Legal Guide for the Visual Artist, Fifth Edition
by Tad Crawford (8 ½ × 11, 280 pages, paperback, $29.95)

Business and Legal Forms for Fine Artists, Third Edition
by Tad Crawford (8 ½ × 11, 176 pages, paperback, $24.95)

Art Without Compromise*
by Wendy Richmond (6 × 9, 256 pages, paperback, $24.95)

Artist's Guide to Public Art: How to Find and Win Commissions
by Lynn Basa (6 × 9, 256 pages, paperback, $19.95)

Selling Art Without Galleries: Toward Making a Living From Your Art
by Daniel Grant (6 × 9, 288 pages, paperback, $24.95)

Fine Art Publicity: The Complete Guide for Galleries and Artists, Second Edition
By Susan Abbott (6 × 9, 192 pages, paperback, $19.95)

How to Start and Run a Commercial Art Gallery
by Edward Winkleman (6 × 9, 256 pages, paperback, $24.95)

The Artist-Gallery Partnership, Third Edition: A Practical Guide to Consigning Art
by Tad Crawford and Susan Mellon (6 × 9, 224 pages, paperback, $19.95)

The Artist's Complete Health and Safety Guide, Third Edition
by Monona Rossol (6 × 9, 416 pages, paperback, $24.95)

Learning by Heart
by Corita Kent and Jan Steward (6 7/8 × 9, 232 pages, paperback, $24.95)

The Quotable Artist
By Peggy Hadden (7 ½ × 7 ½, 224 pages, paperback, $16.95)

Guide to Getting Arts Grants
by Ellen Liberatori (6 × 9, 272 pages, paperback, $19.95)

Caring for Your Art: A Guide for Artists, Collectors, Galleries, and Art Institutions
by Jill Snyder (6 × 9, 192 pages, paperback, $19.95)

Artists Communities: A Directory of Residences that Offer Time and Space for Creativity
by Alliance of Artists Communities (6 × 9, 336 pages, paperback, $24.95)

To request a free catalog or order books by credit card, call 1-800-491-2808. To see our complete catalog on the World Wide Web, or to order online, please visit **www.allworth.com**.